The Silver Domino

The Silver Domino

Marie Corelli

MINT EDITIONS

The Silver Domino was first published in 1892.

This edition published by Mint Editions 2021.

ISBN 9781513277783 | E-ISBN 9781513278193

Published by Mint Editions®

 MINT
EDITIONS

minteditionbooks.com

Publishing Director: Jennifer Newens
Design & Production: Rachel Lopez Metzger
Project Manager: Micaela Clark
Typesetting: Westchester Publishing Services

Contents

I

Openeth Discourse

Well, old musty, dusty, time-trodden arena of Literature and Society, what now? Are your doors wide open, and may a stranger enter? A perpetual dance is going on, so your outside advertisements proclaim; and truly a dance is good so long as it is suggestive of wholesome mirth. But is yours a dance of Death or of Life? A fandango of mockery, a rigadoon of sham, or a waltzing-game at "beggar my neighbour"? Moreover, is the fun worth paying for? Let me look in and judge.

Nay, by the gods of Homer, what a dire confusion of sight and sense and sound is all this "mortal coil" and whirligig of humanity! What noise and laughter, interspersed with sundry groanings, as of fiends in Hell! Listening, I catch the echoes of many voices I know; now and again I have glimpses of faces that in their beauty or ugliness, their smiling or sneering, are perfectly familiar to me. Friends? No, not precisely. No man who has lived long enough to be wise in social wisdom can be certain that he has a friend anywhere; besides, I do not pretend to have found what Socrates himself could not discover. Enemies then? Truly that is probable! Enemies are more than luxuries: they are necessities; one cannot live strongly or self-reliantly without them. One does not forgive them (such pure Christianity has never yet been in vogue); one fights them, and fighting is excellent exercise. So, have at you all, good braggarts of work done and undone! I am as ready to give and take the "passado" as any Mercutio on a hot Italian day. Note or disregard me, I care naught; it is solely for my own diversion, not for yours, that I come amongst you. I want my amusement as others want theirs, and nothing amuses me quite so much as the strange customs and behaviour of the men and women of my time. I love them—in a way; but I cannot, help laughing at them—occasionally. Sentiment would be wasted on them; one does not "grieve" over folly and vice any more, unless one is an ill-paid (and therefore ill-used) cleric, because folly and vice assume such pettifogging and ludicrous aspects that one's risible faculties are at once excited, and pity dries up at its fountain-head. For we live in a little age, and nothing great can breathe in the stifling atmosphere of our languid, listless indifference to God and man.

Nevertheless, there is a curious touch of fantastic buffoonery in everything that temporarily stirs our inertia nowadays. Consider our Browning-mania! Our Stanley-measles! With what dubious and half-bewildered enthusiasm we laid the mortal remains of our incomprehensible "Sordello" to rest in Westminster Abbey! With what vulgar staring and ridiculous parade we gathered together to see the "cute" Welsh trader in ivory wedded to his "Tennant for life" in the same wrongfully-used sacred edifice! Has not our "world of fashion" metaphorically kissed the cow-boots of Buffalo Bill? and "once upon a time," as the fairy-tales say, did not the great true heart of England pour itself out on—Jumbo? A mere elephant, vast of trunk and small of tail—a living representative of our Indian and African possessions; sure 'twas an innocent beast-worship that became us well! What matter if giddy France held her sides with hilarious laughter at us, and Spain and Italy giggled decorously at us behind their fans and mantillas, and Germany broke into a huge guffaw at our "goings-on" over the brim of her beer-mug,—let those laugh who win! And have we not always won? yea, though (in an absent-minded moment) we allowed Barnum, of ever-blessed memory, to buy for vulgar dollars that which we once so loved!

Ah, we are a marvellous and motley crowd at this huge gathering called Life, dear gossips all!—gossips in society and out of society—a motley, lying, hypocritical, crack-brained crowd! I glide in among you, masked for the nonce; I hold my silver draperies well up to my eyes that the smile of derision I now and then indulge in may not show itself too openly. I am not wishful to offend, albeit I am oft offended. Yet it is well-nigh impossible to avoid giving offence in these days. We are like hedgehogs: we bristle at a touch, out of the excess of our hog-like self-consciousness, and the finger of Truth laid on a hair of our skins makes us start with feeble irritability and tetchy nervousness. Christ's command to "bless them that curse you, and pray for them which despitefully use you," is to us the merest feeble paradox; for our detestation of all persons who presume to interfere with our business, and who say unpleasant things about us, is too burningly sincere to admit of discussion. I, for my part, frankly confess to entertaining the liveliest animosity towards certain individuals of my acquaintance, people who shake my hand with the utmost cordiality, smile ingenuously in my eyes, and then go off and write a lying paragraph about me in order to pocket a nefarious half-crown. I never feel disposed to "bless" such folk, and certes, I should be made of flabbier matter than a jelly-fish if I prayed for them.

But then I am not a Christian; please understand that at once. I am a Jew, a Gentile, a Pharisee, and—a devil! I may be all four if I like and yet be Pope of Rome. Why not? since these are the days of free thought, and one's private religious opinions are not made the subject of inquisitorial examination. Moreover, all classes aid and abet the truly pious hypocrite, provided his hypocrisy be strictly consistent. With equal delightsomeness, all creeds, no matter how absurd, just now obtain some kind of a hearing. We are at perfect liberty to worship any sort of fetish we like, without interference. We can grovel before our Divine Self, and sink to the lowest possible level of degradation in ministering to its greedy wants, and yet we shall not for this cause be ostracised from society or excommunicated from any sacred pale. With clerics and with laymen alike, our Divine Self needs more care than our soul's salvation; for our Divine Self, in its splendid egoism, is a breathing, eating, drinking, digesting Necessity; our soul's salvation is a hazy, far-off, dubious concern wherein we are but vaguely interested, a sort of dream at night which we now and then remember languidly in the course of the day.

Talking of dreams, one cannot but consider them with a certain respect. They are such very powerful "factors," as the useful penny-a-liner would say, in the world's history. We affect to despise them; and yet how large a portion of the community are at this moment getting their daily bread-and-butter out of nothing more substantial than the "airy fabric" of a vision, which in this particular instance has proved solid enough to establish itself as one of the foundations of European civilisation.

"The angel of the Lord appeared unto Joseph in a dream."

It is all there. That dream of the good Joseph was the strange nutshell in which lay the germ of all the multitudinous Churches, Popes, Cardinals, Archbishops, bishops, confessors, priests, parsons, and last (not least), curates. One wonders (when one is a doomed and damned "masquer" like myself) what would have happened if Joseph had dreamed a different dream? or, as might have chanced, if he had slept so profoundly as not to have dreamed at all? We should have perhaps been under the sway of Mahomet (another dream), or Buddha (another dream); for certain it is we cannot do without dreams at any period of our lives, from the celebrated "deep sleep" of Adam, when he dreamt he lost a rib to gain a wife, down to the "hypnotic-trance" schools of to-day, where we are gravely informed we can be taught how to murder each other "by suggestion." The most abandoned of us has an Idea—or an Ideal—of something better (or worse) than ourselves, according to whether our daily potations be crushed out of burgundy grape, or made of mere vulgar gin-and-water. Even Hodge, growing stertorous and sleepy over his poisoned beer and *Daily Telegraph* at his favourite "public," takes his turn at castle-building, and drowsily muses on a coming time of Universal Uproar, which *till* it comes is proudly called Socialism, when the "sanguinary" aristocrat will be laid low in the levelling mire, and he, plain Hodge, will be proved a more valuable human unit than any educated ruler of any realm. Alas for thee, good Hodge, that thou should'st boozily indulge in such romantic flights of fancy! Thou, who in uninstructed thirsty haste dost rush to vote for him who most generously plies thee with beer, what would'st thou do without the aristocrat or rich man thou would'st fain trample upon? Who would employ thee, simple Hodge? Another Hodge like thyself? Grant this, and lo! Hodge Number Two, by possessing the means, the will and the power to make thee work for him, tacitly becomes thy master and superior. Wherefore the Equality thou clamourest after, is wholly at an end if thou, Hodge Number One, dost hire thyself out as labourer or servant to Hodge Number Two! This is a plain statement, made plainly, without Gladstonian periods of eloquence; think it over, friend Hodge, when thou art alone, *sans* beer and cheap news-sheet to obfuscate thy simple intelligence.

Nevertheless, it would be cruel to deprive even Hodge of an idea, provided the idea be good for him. For ideas are the only unalterable suggestions of the eternal; their forms change, but themselves are ever the same. One Idea, running through history, built Baal-bec, the Pyramids, the temples of India, the Duomo of Milan, and in our own poor day of brag, the hideous Eiffel tower. The idea has always been the same; to compass great height and vastness of some kind, and Eiffel has only dragged down to the level of his merely mechanical intelligence Nimrod's fantastic notion of the Tower of Babel. Nimrod had a belief that he could reach Heaven. M. Eiffel was convinced he could advertise himself. *Voilà la difference!* That "difference" is the great gulf between ancient art and modern. In the past they went star-gazing and tried to climb—in the present, we stay where we are, look after ourselves, and put up an advertisement. Thus has the form of the idea changed from the likeness of a god into a painted clown—yet, fundamentally, it is still the same idea. And, reduced to its primeval element, its first dim, nebulous hint, an idea is nothing but a dream.

Hence I return to my previous proposition, *i.e.*, the respect we owe to dreams, particularly when they result in fixed realities such as, well!—such as curates, for example. I mention this class of individuals particularly, because there are so many of them, and also because they are generally so desperately poor, and (to young ladies in country parishes) so desperately interesting. What English fiction would do without a curate or a clerical personage of some kind or other to figure in its pages I dare not imagine. The novels of other countries do not produce such hosts of invaluable churchmen, but in England the most successful books are frequently those which treat of the clergy, from "Robert Elsmere," who found himself startled out of orthodoxy by a few familiar and well-ventilated French and German theories of creed, down to the gentle milksops of the church as found in the novels of Anthony Trollope and the dreary stories of Miss Edna Lyall. This well-intentioned lady's productions would assuredly find few readers were it not for the "old-woman-and-faded-spinster" fanaticism for clergymen. And yet—I once knew a wicked army man (worshippers of Edna Lyall prepare to be disgusted! truth is always disgusting) who for some years amused himself by collecting out of the daily newspapers, cuttings of all the police reports and criminal cases in which clergymen were implicated, and this volume, an exceedingly bulky one, he brought to me, with a Mephistophelian twinkle in his bad old eyes.

"Read, mark, learn, and inwardly digest!" said he. "These fellows in 'holy orders' have committed every crime in the calendar, and the only mischief I have not found them out in yet is Arson!"

This was the fact. The calm, unromantic statements of the police, as chronicled in that carefully-collected book of damnatory evidence, bore black witness against clerical virtue and morality—a "reverend" was mixed up in every sort of "abomination" which in old times called down the judgments of the Lord—save and except the one thing—that none of them had been convicted of wilfully setting fire to their own or other peoples' dwellings. But I believe—I may be wrong—that Arson is not a very common crime with any class. It is not of such frequent occurrence as murder or bigamy—or if it is, it does not attract so much attention. So I fancy it may be taken for granted that clergymen are, on the whole, not a whit better, while they are very often worse, than the laity they preach at—hence their "calling and election" is vain, and nobody wonders that they are by their proven inefficiency causing the very pillars of the Church to totter and fall. And has not Parliament been seriously busying itself with a "Clerical Immorality" Bill? This speaks volumes for the integrity of the preachers of the Gospel!

As for me, who am no Churchman, but merely a stray masquerader strolling through the social bazaar, I consider that all churches as they at present exist, are mockeries, and as such, are inevitably doomed. Nothing can save them; no prop will keep them up; neither fancy spiritualism, nor theosophism, nor any other "ism" offered by notoriety-hunting individuals as a stop-gap to the impending crash. Not even the Booth-boom will avail—that balloon of cleverly-inflated philanthropy which has been sent up just high enough to attract attention from the gaping Britishers, who, like big children, must always have something to stare at. Of course, my opinion, being the opinion of an "anonymous," is worthless, and I do not offer it as being valuable. In saying things, I say them for my own amusement, and if I bore any one by my remarks, so much the more am I delighted. As a matter of fact, I take peculiar pleasure in boring people. Why? Because people always bore *me*, and I adore the sentiment of revenge! And that I stand here, masked, a stranger to all the brilliant company whirling wildly around me, is also for my own particular entertainment. If I have said anything to offend any of the excellent clericals I see running towards me with the inevitable "collection-plate," I am sorry. But I will not bribe them for their good opinion, nor will I flatly disobey the command received (which they all seem to forget), "Do not your alms before men." Besides, I have nothing with me just now—not a farthing. I am only in this great assembly for a few moments, and my "silver domino," lavishly studded with stars, has cost me dear. For the completion of churches, and the mending of chancels, and the french-polishing of pews, I have no spare cash. Walls will not hold me when I am fain to worship—I take the whole arching width of the uncostly sky. There are rich old ladies in this vast throng of people, doubtless?—dear Christian souls who hate their younger relatives, and who are therefore willing to spend spare cash in order to prove their love of God. From these gather your harvest while you may, all ye ordained "disciples of the Lord," but excuse a poor wandering Nobody from No-land from the uncongenial task of helping to provide a new organ for parish yokels, and from sending out cheap Bibles to the "heathen Chinee," who frequently disdains to read them. Let me pass on—I am not worth buttonholing—and I want to take a passing glance at things in general. I shall whisper, mutter, or talk loudly about anything I see, just as the humour takes me. Only I will not promise any polite lying. Not because I object to it, but simply because it has become commonplace. Everybody does it, and thus it has ceased to be original, or even diplomatic. To openly declare the Truth—the truth of what we are now, and what, in the course of our present down-hill "progress," we are likely to become; the truth that is incessantly and relentlessly gnawing away at the foundations of all our social sophistries—to do this, I say, and stand by it when done, would be the only possible novelty that could really startle the indolent and exhausted age. But nobody will undertake it. It would be too troublesome. One would run so many risks. One would offend so many "nice" people! True—very true. All the same, neither for convenience nor amiability do I personally consider myself bound to tell lies for the mere sake of lying. So, while elbowing a passage through the crowd, I shall give expression to whatever thoughts occur to me, inconsequentially or rationally, as my varying moods suggest; moreover, I shall be very content to glide out of the "hurly-burly," and enter it no more, when once I have said my say.

II

Soliloquiseth on Little Manners

One can hardly be among a great number of people more or less distinguished, without observing the way they move, talk, walk, and generally behave themselves. And the first impression received on entering the throng over which the electric light flashes its descriptive sky-sign "Present Day" is distinctly one of—bad manners; yes, bad, ungainly, jostling, "higgledy-piggledy" manners. The general effect (bird's-eye view) is as of motley-clothed lunatics hurrying violently along to a land of Nowhere. Men stoop and shuffle and amble from the knees, instead of walking with an erect and dignified demeanour; women skip or waddle, making thereby an undue exhibition of purely English feet. In art-collections one sees plenty of old engravings wherein are depicted gallant, well-shaped gentlemen, pressing three-cornered hats to the left sides of their lace-ruffled, manly bosoms, and bending with exquisite deference and stately deportment to demurely sweet dames, who, holding out gossamer skirts in taper fingers, perform the prettiest curtsies in response. It must have been charming to see them thus habitually realising the value of mutual politeness in everyday life; one would like to witness a revival of the same. Men lost nothing by outwardly expressing a certain reverence for women; women gained a great deal by outwardly expressing their gentle acknowledgment of that reverence. "Manner makyth the man," says the old adage, and if that be true, then there are no men, for certainly there are no manners—at least, not among the "upper ten." I am in a position to judge, for I am somewhat of a favourite at Court, where manners are not at a very high premium. I can only judge, of course, by what I see, and in my observations of the fair sex I submit that, not being a "fair" myself, I may be wrong. Yet I believe it is true that ladies of high rank and good education are obliged to be taught (three lessons for one guinea) how to make a proper obeisance to the Queen. And the lesson is, I presume, too cheap to include any training in the art of decently polite behaviour during the "wait" before entering the Throne-room. The impudent push and self-assertion of these "noble dames" is something amazing to witness: the looks at one another—looks as bold as those of Jezebel—

the scramble, the reckless tearing of lace, and scratching of arms and shoulders in the heated *mêlée* is—well—simply degrading to the very name of womanhood. Better, dear ladies, not to go to a Drawing-room at all if you cannot get to your Queen without tearing your fellow-woman's dress off her back and inflicting scars on her unprotected shoulders. Men are better behaved at the *levées*, but among them all scarce one knows how to bow. Nevertheless, they are more polite to each other than women are; they are obliged to be—no man will take insolence from another man without instantly resenting it.

A strange thing it is to consider how poets have raved from time immemorial about the "grace" of woman! It is pathetic to see how these ingenuous verse-writers will persist in keeping up their illusions. As a matter of fact, in England at least, there is scarce one woman in a hundred who knows how to walk well. And that one is always such a "peculiar" object that her movements are generally commented upon as "affected." To a masculine observer this is very strange. A lady who bundles up her clothes well behind, exposes thick legs, flat feet, and ugly boots all at once in order to effect her entrance into carriage, cab, or omnibus, is, by certain of her own sex, voted "a good soul," "unaffected," "no nonsense about her," "as frank and simple a creature as ever lived." But a lady who lifts her dress just high enough to show the edge of a dainty lace on her petticoat, clean, trim boots, the suspicion of an ankle, and only the pleasing suggestion of a leg—she—ah! nasty designing creature! "No good, my dear!" "all affectation, every bit of her!" *"Look at the lace on her petticoat!"* This last clause, I have noticed, is always damnatory in the opinion of super-excellent females with no lace on their petticoats. There is enough in this suggestion to make even a strolling masquerader pause and meditate, because, arguing from the point of view taken by many eminently virtuous dames, it would seem that manners, *i.e.*, walking well, keeping clean, and holding one's self with a certain affable grace and air of distinction, are indicative of latent cunning. This curious but popular fallacy applies in England to men as well as women. The awkward gawk, whose clothes never fit, and who appears to be always encumbered and distressed by his own hands and feet, is frequently declared to be a "good fellow," "heart in the right place," "regular trump," and so forth, as probably he is. I do not for a moment imply that he is not. But I will maintain that because a man holds himself well, dresses well, and is perfectly at ease with the appurtenances of his own body, he need not therefore be "a confirmed *roué*" "a turf man," or "a club gamester." But this is what he frequently passes for if he dares to indulge in a suspicion of "manner." In fact, the only presumable effort of "style" now attempted by the men of to-day appears to be concentrated in the art of twirling or stroking the moustache whenever the owner of the moustache perceives a pretty woman. This little trick is done in different ways, of course; the "twist" can be rendered insolently, familiarly, aggressively, or with a caressing feline movement, indicative of dawning amorousness. It is frequently effective, particularly with schoolgirls and provincial misses, who have been known to render up their susceptible hearts instantaneously to one victorious twirl of a really well-grown moustache, but I have also seen many creditable performances of moustache-twirling completely thrown away on unappreciative women. It is, however, the only piece of elegance—if elegance it can be called—indulged in by the true "masher." And beyond it he never soars. He does not know how to lift his hat gracefully; he does not know how to enter a room (without looking vaguely surprised or beamingly idiotic), or leave it again with any touch of affable dignity. His movements are generally stiff and ungainly to the very last degree, and, worst of all, he seldom has any brains to make up for his lack of breeding.

A good position from whence to observe the manners of the time is close to the right hand of the Premier on the evening of a great crush at the Foreign Office. If courtly Lord Salisbury be there, you get in his bow, smile, and cordial handshake the finest essence of diplomatic urbanity and ease. But when you have exchanged greetings with him and his gracious lady you have seen nearly all you shall see of "manner." The throng come tumbling in helter-skelter, treading on each other's heels, for all the world like an untrained crowd of the "bas-peuple," all heated, all flustered, all vaguely staring ahead. Ambassadors, foreign princes, military dignitaries, jerk their heads spasmodically on entering the rooms, but evidently have no proper notion of a bow, while some of them let their arms hang stiffly down at their sides, and proffer a salutation that seems as though it were the result of a galvanic wire working their spines by some curious patent process not yet quite perfected. And the women!—the poets' goddesses! They arrive in very ungoddess-like bundles of rich clothing, some waddling, some ambling, some sidling, but only a rare few, a dozen at most, *walking*, or carrying themselves as being at all superior to their gowns. Most of these "fair" forget to curtsey properly to their distinguished entertainers, and the general impression made on the mind of an observer in looking at the "manner" of their entrance is distinctly unpleasing. Most of them wear far too many diamonds, a notable sign of egregious bad taste. A woman I saw there on one occasion wore a sort of dish-cover of diamonds on her head. (A friend told me it was a "garland"; it may have been, but it looked like a dish-cover.) Her hair was straight and flat, and stuck close to her scalp, and beneath the gorgeous headpiece of jewels was a fat red face profusely adorned with wrinkles and pimples, on which the diamonds cast a cruel glare. "Alas, good soul," I thought, as she went glittering past, "thou hast fallen on the most evil hour of all thy span— the fateful time when thy jewels are preferable to thyself!"—though, truly, as an unnoteworthy personage, I may here remark that I do not like diamonds. I own that a few choice stones, finely set and sparkling among old lace, are effective, but the woman who can wear a soft white gown without any ornaments save natural flowers would always carry away the palm of true distinction for me. I confess my notions are old-fashioned, especially those concerning women.

Talking of the Foreign Office, there was a terrible man there once who trod on everybody's toes. He seemed born to do it. He was tall and powerful, and wore the full Highland costume. I shall never forget the bow he made to Lady Salisbury—it bent him double in true Scottish fashion; for a *bonâ-fide* Scot, you know, always yearns to cast himself on his knees before a title. It is in his blood and heritage so to do: the remains of the old humility practised by the clans to their chiefs what time they were all robbers and rievers together. This man literally divided himself to do fitting homage to the Premier's lady—his head sank to the level of the hem of her dress, while the back part of his kilt (not to be irreverent) rose visibly in air in a way that was positively startling. The achievement appeared to alarm some people, to judge by their anxious looks. Would the noble Highlander ever come straight again? That was the question that was evidently agitating the observers of his attitude. He did come straight, with galvanic suddenness too, and marched off on the war-path through the rooms, planting his foot, not "on his native heath," but on every other foot he could find with a manly disregard of consequences. He was a great man, he *is* a great man; I feel sure he must be, otherwise he would not have hurt so many people without apologising.

As a matter of fact, there is nothing so rare in these days as distinguished and affable manners. An Arab thief has often more external personal dignity than many an English peer. In some of the best houses in the land I have seen the owners of the stately surroundings comport themselves with such awkward sheepishness as to suggest the idea that they were there by mistake. I have seen great ladies sitting in their own drawing-rooms with a fidgety and anxious air, as though they momentarily expected to be ordered out by their paid domestics. When I was "green" and new to society I used to think somewhat of dukes and earls. I had a foolish notion that the wearers of great historic names must somehow look as if they inwardly felt the distinction of race and ancestry. Now that I know a great many of these titled folk, I have discovered my mistake. I find several of them vote their "ancestors" a "bore." They carry no outward marks to show that they ever had ancestors. They might indeed have been ground into existence by means of a turning-lathe, for aught of inherited beauty, stateliness or courtesy they exhibit. I have seen great dukes bulge into a room with less grace than sacks of flour, and I have watched "belted earls" sneaking timorously after the footman who announced their lofty names, with a guilty air as though they had picked that footman's plush pockets on the way. I once heard a very, very "blue-blooded" duchess run through the items of her chronic indigestion with as much weight and emphasis of detail as a brandy-seeking cook. A famous lord, brother to a famous duke, has shuffled into my study and sunk into a chair with the "manner" of an escaped convict, and I have had much ado to drag him out of his self-evident humiliation. He has picked his fingers and surveyed his boots disconsolately. He has felt the leg of his trouser in doubtful plight. That his "ancestry" performed acts of valour on Bosworth field awakens in his flabby soul no pulse of pride. His heroic progenitors might as well have been tallow-chandlers for all he cares. Yet he is the living representative of their greatness, more's the pity! I often wonder what those old Bosworth fellows would say if they could come to life and see him—their descendant—as he is—with but two ideas in his distinguished noddle—ballet-girls and brandy-and-soda!

I am here reminded of an incident which in this place may not come amiss. I happened to be present on one occasion at a luncheon-party made up chiefly of men, most of them well known in Parliament and society. Our hostess was (and is) a lady who always has more men than women at her parties, but on this particular day there was one stranger present, a lady noted for a great literary success. After luncheon, when this lady took leave of her hostess and went downstairs into the hall, it was found that her carriage had not arrived. She waited patiently, with the footman on guard staring at her. Meanwhile man after man came downstairs, passed her in the hall as though she were a stray servant (they had all eagerly conversed with her at luncheon, and had tried to get as much entertainment out of her as possible), and never uttered a word. Not one of them paused to say, "Allow me to escort you upstairs till your carriage comes," or, "Can I do anything for you?" or, "May I have the pleasure of waiting to see you into your carriage?" or any other of the old-world chivalrous formalities once *de rigueur* with every gentleman. Not one man; except the last who came down, and who (under the immediate circumstances) shall be nameless, as he was evidently a fool. Because among the gentlemen who thus passed the lady by, were Lord Randolph Churchill, Mr. Lockwood, Q.C., and other "notabilities," so I am forced to argue from this that it is the very essence of modern "good form" to ignore a lady (with whom you have previously conversed) at the precise moment when she might seem to require a little attention. So that the stupid and ill-bred person was the nameless "he" who came down last, who spoke to the solitary "damozel," escorted her upstairs again to her hostess, waited with her, chatting pleasantly in the drawing-room till her carriage arrived, then took her down to it, put her in, and lifted his hat respectfully as she drove away. He was not "nineteenth-century form"—and his "manner" was obsolete. Most people would rather be considered downright vulgar than what they are pleased to term "old-fashioned."

Hurry kills "manner," and there can be no doubt that in this day we are all in a frantic hurry. I don't know what about, I'm sure. We are after no good that I can see. I have tried to fathom the reason of this extraordinary and vilely unbecoming haste, and the only apparent cause I can discover is that we are trying to get as much out of life as possible before we die. The means, however, entirely defeat the object. We have no time to be generous, no time to be sympathetic, no time to converse well, no time to do anything but feed and look after our own interests, and we get so fatigued in the business of living that life itself becomes worthless. At least, so it seems to me. I say we are "all" in a terrible hurry, but this is not quite correct. There are exceptions to the rule. I myself am one. I never hurry. I "laze" through life and enjoy it. I never "scramble" for anything, and never "fluster" myself for anybody. Even now I am sauntering, not rushing, amidst you all with the utmost ease; I move softly and talk softly, and, though frequently disposed to laughter,

I never snigger aloud. The loud snigger (sign of "well-bred" hilarity) is the muffled but exact echo of the donkey's bray. It resembles it in tone and sense and quality. I avoid it; because, though a donkey is an exceedingly clever beast and much maligned, his voice might be easily surpassed. As it is, *au naturel*, it does not appear to me worth imitating.

And now, pardon me, sirs and dames, but as I perceive a small crowd of you engaged in the truly English occupation of staring, not at me, but at my glittering domino, and as I do not wish to create an obstruction, I will, with your very good leave, pass on. Observe how quietly I glide; with only the very faintest rustle of my "star-spangled" wrappings; striving not to tread on anybody's corns, carefully winding my way in and out the busy throng, and only holding myself a little more erect than some of you, because—well! because I have no favours to ask of anybody, and therefore need not trouble myself to acquire the nineteenth-century skulk and propitiatory grin. And so—on through the motley!

III

Pronounceth on Lesser Morals

I think if everybody would only be as frank as I am, they would confess we haven't such a thing as a Little Moral left, except in the copybooks. Big Morals are everywhere, writ large for all the world to see; we don't trouble about them because they do not individually concern us—they are merely the names and forms that help to keep things going. But little morals are gone out of fashion entirely. It is rather perplexing when we come to think of it. Because we ought to be moral, strictly moral; and feeling that we ought to be, we have to pretend that we are. Sometimes we find it difficult to keep up the game, but as a rule we succeed fairly well. Only we know, you know, that a "little moral" is a bore. That is why, in our heart of hearts, we will have nothing to do with it. For example, it is not on the lines of "little morality" that we should run up bills. But we do run them up. Sometimes, too, without the smallest intention of paying them. It is not in the path of unselfish virtue that we should give our dear friends wine from the "stores" at "store" prices, while we carefully reserve our old Chambertin and Chateau d'Yquem for our own special drinking; but we do this sort of thing every day. And yet we love our dear friends—oh! how we love them! we would do anything for them, anything—except produce our Chambertin. And it is not, I believe, a "little moral," *i.e.*, a copybook maxim, that we should fall in love with our neighbour's wife. But that is just precisely the most delightful among our modern fashionable amusements. Our neighbour's wife is the most interesting woman in our social set. Our neighbour's daughter is not half so interesting. Because our neighbour's daughter is generally marriageable; our neighbour's wife is only divorceable—hence her superior charm. The scandalous and rude statement, "Whoso looketh on his neighbour's wife to lust after her, hath already committed—" No, no! I will not defile delicate ears polite with pure New Testament language. It is too strong; it is painfully strong—quite unpleasant—a thunderous speech uttered by the holiest lips that ever breathed man's breath, but it is shocking, and gives our nerves an unpleasant thrill. Because we do look after our neighbour's wife a good deal nowadays; "neigh" after her is the old Scriptural term for our latter-day custom, which has been set in vogue by the most distinguished examples of aristocracy among us. And our neighbour's wife's husband is a capital butt for our "chaff"; we like him, oh yes, we always like him: we go and stay with him for weeks, and shoot game in his preserves, and ride his best horses; he is a capital fellow, by Jove, but an awful fool. Yes, so he is. Our neighbour's wife's husband is generally a fool. His dense noddle never discerns any way out of his dishonour but the crooked path of the law. I haven't got a wife—praise be to heaven!—but if I had, and I found any "noble" personage disposed to "neigh" after her, I know what I should do with him. I should trounce him with a tough cowhide thong till his "blue blood" declared itself, till his "nobility" roared for mercy. Whether he were prince, duke, lord, or plain "Mister," he would be black as well as "blue" before I had done with him. Of course the law would have to come in afterwards by way of a summons for assault, but who would not pay liberally for the satisfaction of thrashing a low scoundrel? Besides, viewed in the most practical light, it would cost less than the business of divorce, besides having the immense advantage of giving no satisfaction to the guilty parties concerned.

By Heaven, there are some men I know whom I would kick in the way of pure friendship, if a kick would rouse them to a sense of their position—men whose wives are openly shamed, the whole public knowing of their flagrant, unblushing infidelity—men who stand by and look on at their own disgrace, and yet presume to offer the "example" of a public career to the "lower" classes. And how these "lower" despise them; how they who still do call a spade a spade are filled with honest scorn for such "distinguished" cowards! Well, well, I shall do no good, I warrant, by heating my blood in the cause of the worthless and degraded; fidelity in wives, manly principle in husbands, are "little morals," and seem to have gone out with the jewelled snuff-boxes and rapiers of old time.

Among other of these "little morals" it used to be tacitly understood that "gentlemen" should preserve a certain delicacy of speech when conversing before "ladies." This idea appears to be almost obsolete. Men have no scruple nowadays in talking about their special ailments to women (and not old women either), and they will allude to the various parts of their bodies affected by those ailments in the most frankly disgusting manner. At a supper-party given by one of the most exalted of noble dames not long ago, I heard a brute detailing the ins

MARIE CORELLI

and outs of his "liver" trouble to an embarrassed looking young woman of about eighteen. As for the ugly word "stomach," it is commonly used in various circles of the *beau-monde*, and the most revolting details of medicine and surgery are frequently dealt with in what used to be termed "polite conversation." That ugly old women, and fat, greasy matrons love to chatter about their own and their friends' illnesses, is of course an accepted fact, but that men should do so before a casual company of the married and unmarried "fair" is a new and highly repulsive phase of "social intercourse." I remember hearing the editor of a well-known magazine talk with a pretty young unmarried woman concerning the possibilities of her sex in Art, and after the utterance of many foolish platitudes, he brought his remarks to a brusque conclusion with the following words: "Oh yes, I admire gifted women, but, after all, their genius is bound to be interfered with and marred by the *bearing of children*." Coarse ruffian as he was, I suppose the surprised, hot blush that stained the poor girl's face was agreeable to his low little soul, while I, for my part, yearned to knock him down. His words, and above all, his manner, implied that he in his fatuous mind considered every woman bound, willy-nilly, to submit herself to the passions of man, be she saint or sinner. "The bearing of children," as he put it, is, according to natural animal law, the prime business of the average woman's life, average women being seldom fit for anything else. But it has to be conceded that there are women above the average, who, gifted with singular powers of ambition and attainment, sweep on from one intellectual triumph to another, and do so succeed in quelling the natural animalism that they do not consider themselves bound to "bring forth and multiply" their kind. With brilliant, fiery-souled Bashkirtseff, they exclaim: "Me marier et avoir des enfants! Mais chaque blanchisseuse peut en faire autant!"

And in her next sentence the captive genius cries: "Mais qu'est ce que je veux? Oh, vous le savez bien. Je veux la gloire!" And "la gloire," despite the opinions of the vulgar little editor aforementioned, does not precisely consist in having babies, in hushing their frantic yells hour after hour, and wiping their perpetually dribbling noses, what time the fathers of these "blessings" sleep and snore in peace. "La gloire" assumes an inviting aspect to many feminine souls to-day, and the "joys of marriage" pale in comparison. It is rather a dangerous seed to sow, this "la gloire," in the hitherto tame fields of woman's life and labour, and the harvest promises to astonish the whole world. That is, provided women will be original and not imitate men. At present they imitate us too closely, and even in the question of coarse freedom of speech they ape the masculine example. If a man insists on talking about his "liver" a woman will bring her "leg" into the conversation in order to be even with him. The vulgar word "ripping" slips off the tongue of a well-bred young woman as easily as though she were a rough schoolboy. And so on through the whole gamut of slang. As a casually interested spectator of these things, I would respectfully inform the "fair" that as long as they elect to "follow" instead of "lead," so long will their efforts to attain eminence be laughed at and contemptuously condemned. A painful flabby-mindedness distinguishes many of the sex feminine, an inviting readiness to be "sat upon" which is perhaps touching, but also ridiculous. If you take up an art, dear ladies, you require to be strong if you ever wish to consummate anything worth doing. Art accepts no half measures. You will need to live solitary and eat the bread of bitterness, with tears for wine. Consolations you will have doubtless, but they will come slowly, and not from without, only from within. An ethereal ice-air will surround and sever you from the common lot, you will be lifted higher and higher into a cold, pure atmosphere that will require all your force of lung to breathe without losing life in the effort. If you can stand it—well! if not, better be Bashkirtseff's "blanchisseuse qui pent faire autant."

Is it worth while, among "little morals," to mention gambling? I trow not? Everybody gambles, from the men on the Stock Exchange to the princes of the blood. We gamble on the turf, in the clubs, and in our own homes, with the most admirable persistency. Any trifling excuse serves, as, for example, a man asked me the other day to risk a sovereign on the question as to whether a certain music-hall artiste's Christian name began with a P. or a W. I declined the offer, not being interested in music-hall artistes. And this brings me to a final point in our "little morals," namely, the point of considering how utterly and finally some of us have kicked over the traces with regard to preserving the respectability and virtue of our women. We frequently allow women to do things nowadays that may, or will, in the end degrade them, while we put obstacles in all directions to retard their elevation to distinction in the arts or sciences. We hate the idea of their having a voice in the government of the country, but we do not at all mind their appearing half naked to dance before us on the stage. We are hardly civil to the young daughters of our aristocratic host, but we will make a countess of the public dancer of "break-downs." We will only arrive at an intimate friend's ball in time to eat his supper, but we will hang about for hours to stare at an advertised "beauty barmaid." Yet I should not say "we," since I am not guilty of these things. I am not fond of music-halls, though I confess to finding them more entertaining than Mr. Irving's hydraulic efforts at tragedy. Still I daresay my good friend Gladstone patronises them more than I do. Again, I am not devoted to barmaids. I may here remark a trifling particular connected with "little morals" which has often struck me. It is this. A "man about town" will kiss a pretty housemaid or any other "low-class" woman he fancies without considering himself demeaned by the act. Now, how is it that a lady of equal position never wishes to kiss a footman or a waiter at a restaurant? One would think the situation as tempting to one sex as another. But no. The "lady" would consider herself insulted if kissed by a footman; the "gentleman" chuckles with ecstasy if kissed by the housemaid. Why is this thus? I am inclined to think that here the "fair sex" score the winning number in the trifling matter of self-respect.

And now we have come soundly upon the cause of our open disregard of "little morals." It is this: loss of self-respect. We do not respect ourselves any longer, probably because we do not find ourselves worthy of respect. We cannot respect a creature who is ready to sell soul, body, sentiment, and opinion for hard cash, but that creature is Ourself, in this blessed time of progress. Morals are nowhere weighed against a fat balance at the banker's. Self-respect is ridiculous if it opposes the gospel of Grab. What will self-respect do for us? Simply isolate us from our fellow-men! Our fellow-men tell convenient lies, cheat prettily, steal their neighbour's wives, and yet walk openly in social daylight; why should not we all do the same? Where is the harm? We only hurt ourselves if we try to do otherwise, and, what is far worse, we are looked upon as fools. We cannot possibly be "in the swim" unless we are good hypocrites. Herein is my sore point. I am unable to hypocrise. Candour is part of my composition. It is unfortunate, because it keeps me out of many delightful entertainments where Humbug rules the roast. Socrates was not a "social" favourite, neither am I. I am perfectly aware how unpleasantly tedious I have been all the time I have talked about morals. They are not interesting subjects of conversation at any time, and people would much rather not hear about them at all. True! Only in church o' Sundays are we bound (by fashion's decree) to listen to discourses on morality by a possibly immoral cleric, but during the week we are, thank Heaven, free to forget that morals, little or big, exist. This is as it should be in all civilised communities. Of course we must keep up the *pretence* of morality—this is a necessity enforced by law and police. But we may piously assure ourselves that our "feigning" is the most perfectly finished art in the world. No nation can out-rival the English in Sunday-show morality. It is the severest, grandest, dullest Sham ever evolved from social history. From its magnitude it commands wondering admiration; from its ludicrous inconsistency it provokes laughter. And I, strolling idler as I am, stop an instant to stare and smile, and involuntarily I think of the Ten Commandments. I believe that on one occasion Moses was so angry that he broke the tablets on which they were graven. This was mere temper on the part of Moses; he should have known better. He should have spared the tablets, and broken the Commandments, every one of them; as we do!

IV

OF SAVAGES AND SKELETONS

P ausing awhile to consider the question, I find that on the whole, most of you, my dear friends, appear to get on excellently well without either manners or morals. There you all are, taking your several parts in the pageant before me, pushing, scrambling, and making generally the most infernal din, the while you move heaven and earth to serve your own personal interest and pleasure, regardless of anybody else's convenience, and you manage to make a tolerably good show of respectability. Your finished education in the great art of counterfeiting does everything for you. The sum and substance of modern culture is in the one line, "Assume a virtue though you have it not." You all "assume" superbly. And yet the best actors tell us they find their profession entails fatigue and exhaustion at times, and they are glad when they can throw aside the mask and take to "rough-and-tumble" in the secrecy of their own homes. For there is one great fact about us which we all strive to hide, and yet which is for ever declaring itself, and that is, that despite all our civilisation and progress, we are savages still. Absolute barbarians are we, born so, made so, and neither God nor Time shall alter us. Our education teaches us how to cover Nature with a mask, even as our innocent Scriptural progenitors covered themselves with fig-leaves; but Nature is not thereby destroyed. The savage leaps out at all sorts of times and seasons, in the tempers and habits of the most highly cultured men and women. "My Lord," unbracing himself at night and unbuttoning his waistcoat to give freedom to his ample paunch, hiccoughs himself into bed with as much rude noise as the naked Zulu who has drunk himself nearly dead on rum. "My Lady," unclasping her fashionable "corset" and allowing her beauties to expand, sighs, yawns, shakes herself jelly-wise in freedom, and plumps between the sheets as casually as any squaw in a wigwam. And it is probable that both my lord and my lady asleep, snore as loudly and look as open-mouthed and ugly in their slumbers as any uncivilised brutes ever born. Old Carlyle's notion of the virtue of clothes was the correct one. What should we do with a naked Parliament? The clothes maintain order and respectability, but without artificial covering the whole community would be as they truly are in their heart of hearts—savages, and no more.

I think we are all pretty well conscious of this, some of us perhaps painfully so. And what we are painfully aware of we always try to conceal. Byron, despite his genius, was always thinking of his club-foot. So are we always voluntarily or involuntarily, thinking of our savagery. It will out, still, as I say, we do try to keep it in. We do most faithfully pretend we are civilised, though we know we never shall be; not in this planet. The thing is manifestly impossible. The attraction of sex, the love of fighting, the thirst of conquest, the greed of power: these things are savage elements, like wind and fire and lightning; they make up life, and so long as life is ours, so long shall we be savages at heart—savages in our grandest passions as well as in our meanest. That is why I am disposed to think the doctrines of Christianity unsuited to the world, because they are so directly opposed to natural instinct. However, this is a point I am quite unfitted to argue upon, being of no creed myself, and very much of a savage to boot. Personally, I would not give a fig for a man who had nothing of the savage about him. I have met the kind of fellow often, especially among the literary set. "Not that I intend to imply," as the G. O. M. sayeth, "that under certain circumstances, and given certain conditions," the literary set cannot be savage—they can be, and are, but it is a savagery that is mere palaver, and never comes to honest fisticuffs. The "literary set" are physically timorous, and not fond of firearms or manly sports; effeminacy and dyspepsia mark these gifted creatures for their own. They have "nerves," have the bookish folk, like fine ladies, and with the "nerves" spite and petulance go as a matter of course. Real, *bonâ-fide*, fierce savagery is infinitely preferable to the puling whine or the cynical snarl of little poets and "society" philosophers; and the company of a bluff soldier who has "faced fire" is preferable to that of a dozen magazine editors.

Gathering my domino closer about me, I gaze steadily over the circling noisy throng that whirls before me, and I think of wild tribes and famished hordes scurrying fiercely along through clouds of sand over miles of desert, and I see very little difference between the "cultured" crowd and the hungry "barbarians." Desert, or the road called Custom; sand or dust in the eyes of moral perception—they come to very much the same thing in the end. Can it be possible that the present century is "helping on" civilisation? I don't believe it any more than I believe that the wretches who flung themselves under the car of

MARIE CORELLI

Juggernaut went straight to heaven. The most curious and awful part of the whole spectacle to me is to realise that all this movement, clamour, and confusion, should be doomed to end in sudden silence by and by; such silence, that not a sound from any one of these now living noisy tongues will stir it by so much as a curse or a groan.

Yes, my friends; deny it if you will that we are all savages (I expect you to deny it because I assert it, and you would not be human if you did not contradict me), you will hardly refuse to admit that we are all skeletons. Our flesh makes our savagery. Our clothes make our morality. But reduced to our primal selves, we are plain Bones. And in honest, unadorned Bones, to be positive to the utmost degree of positivism, we invariably discover ourselves grinning. At what? Ah, who shall say! Unless it be at our own exquisite fooling with fate, which, truth to tell, is very exquisite indeed. And, however serious we may look in the flesh, we must remember our own death's-head is always laughing at us.

Death's-heads are jolly companions. Some of my friends are fond of wearing imitation ones to remind them of the wide perpetual smile they carry behind their own fleshly covering. One or two charming ladies I know carry jewelled death's-heads on their watch-chains, and play with them in a sufficiently gruesome manner. Lady Dorothy Nevill, she of shrewd Walpole wit and keen intelligence, wears a conspicuous ornament given her by our own amiable Prince of Wales—a red coral or cornelian death's-head, with a couple of diamonds in the eye-sockets. I wonder what Albert Edward was thinking about when he made the lady this valuable present, and whether the line, "To this complexion must we come at last," occurred at all to his memory. Lady Dorothy herself is particularly fond of the suggestive bauble; she perceives and appreciates as much as I do the delicate irony of a skull's smile.

And it really needs a good deal of intelligence to understand death's-heads. A duke I know, of the best possible ducal brand, annoys me exceedingly by his lack of perception in this regard. The handle of his walking-stick is an ivory skull, and he is always sucking it. The effect of this act is indescribable. He seems to be mouthing the dried and polished cranium of an ancestor. I meet him frequently in the "row," or Snobs' Parade, where gilded youth goes to stare at gilded age, by which phrase I mean that the foot-passengers are mostly young and lissom of limb, while the fine carriages frequently contain naught but the dried and desolate fragments of old age, or the painted and bedizened wrecks of youth. It is really quite curious to note how few pretty or even genial-looking persons are seen in the vehicles that crowd the Row during a "season." Max O'Rell declares that the entire show is like Tussaud's wax-work taken out for an airing, but I have never seen any one so good-looking or so clear-complexioned as wax-work in a carriage. On foot, yes; there are any number of pretty women and tolerably well set-up men to be met with strolling about under the trees, and it is precisely for this reason that whenever I go to the Park I walk instead of driving, as I prefer pretty women to ugly ones.

And thus by preamble and general tedium I have come leisurely round to the point I wished to arrive at, which is the narration of a singular dream I once had; a vision which fell upon me, not in the "silence of the night," but in the glaring heat of a midsummer afternoon while I was seated on a penny chair in the middle of the Row. I had just exchanged the usual greetings with my kindly young idiot friend the duke (sucking the ivory skull on his cane as usual) and he had gone on his way blandly grinning. I had shaken hands with a couple of vagrant journalists. I had saluted a few charming women, chatted for ten minutes with Lord Salisbury, and had imparted to a dear paunchy diplomat the secret of stewing prawns in wine—a dish which I assure you, on the faith of a true *gourmet*, is excellent. I had studied the back of a massively fat woman's dress for several seconds, trying to puzzle out the ways and means by which it got fastened over so much rebellious flesh. Fatigued with these exertions, and lulled by the monotonous noise of the rolling wheels of the carriages going to and fro, I fell into a sort of semi-conscious doze, in which I was perfectly aware of my surroundings, though more than half asleep. And "a change came o'er the spirit" of the scene—a change which might have alarmed unphilosophic people, but which to one like myself, who am surprised at nothing, merely transformed a dull and ordinary spectacle into a deeply interesting one. A curious white light pervaded the atmosphere and tinged the overhanging foliage with a sickly shade of green, the yellow sunshine took upon itself a jaundiced hue, and lo! all suddenly and straightway the "row" was stripped of its "too, too solid flesh" and appeared as too, too truthful Bones. Bones were the fashion of the hour—skulls the order of the day. Clothes were worn, of course, for decency's sake, clothes, too, of the very newest fashion and cut; but flesh was discarded as superfluous. And so the most elegant Paris "creations" in the way of lace parasols shaded the sun from the delicate female death's-heads; skeleton steeds in gorgeous trappings worked their ribs bravely, guided along by skeleton coachmen superb in plush and wigs well powdered; and dear antiquated Lady Doldrums, as she turned her eye-sockets to right and left with a pleasant leer, seemed to be more cheerful than she had been for many a long day. She still wore her favourite style of youthful hat, pinched artistically about the brim and turned up with artificial roses, but these handsomely-made French flowers now nodded quite waggishly against her bare jaws, knowing there was no longer any painted flesh there to eclipse their colour. Yes, Lady Doldrums was herself at last—the terrible strain of pretending to be young was over, and the only *coquetterie* she practised in her honest condition of Bones, was the wielding of a fan in her grisly sticks of fingers, not for heat's sake—no, merely to keep away the flies. And the wonderful crowd thickened every moment—bones, bones, nothing but bones;—they multiplied by scores, and I began to find out a few of my dear society friends by the armorial bearings on their carriages. I could guess nothing by their faces, as these were nearly all alike, and there was no variety of expression. True, there were short jaws and long, high foreheads and low, wide skulls and narrow, but I was unable to guide myself entirely by these hints. I found out Randolph Churchill, though, in a minute, but then his head is of a curious shape one does not easily forget. I should know his skull anywhere as thoroughly as the gravedigger in *Hamlet* knew Yorick's. He looked very cool and comfortable in his bones, I thought. So did the delightful *danseuse* who followed close behind him in a high-wheeled trap, with the smartest little skeleton "tiger" possible to conceive, pranked out in livery, an impudent little top-hat perched jauntily on his impudent little half-grown skull, while as for the exquisite "dancing-girl" herself, good heavens! her bones were positively fascinating! The wind whistled in and out them with a breezy amorousness—and then her smile was more than usually perfect owing to the admirable set of false teeth which were so dexterously screwed into her jaw. It would take years of mouldering away to loosen those teeth, and the mouldering had evidently not yet begun. She wore a wig too—a bronze-red wig in beauteous curl—and upon my soul, she looked almost as well arrayed in bones as in her usual heavily enamelled flesh. Very different was the aspect of the toothless old bundle that came after, seated in a springy victoria, and wrapped in rich rugs to the chin. His skeleton steeds pranced nobly, his skeleton coachman sat stiffly upright, his skeleton footman preserved the accustomed dignified cross-armed attitude, but he himself, poor wretch, rolled uneasily from side to side, till it seemed that his yellow skull would sever itself from the spinal attachment and fall incontinently into his own shaking claws. I recognised him by the showy monogram on his carriage-rug; he was the rich proprietor of several newspapers, the "impresario" of several music-halls, and the dotard lover of several ballet-girls. After him came a "four-in-hand," a marvellous sight to see with its skeleton team, its "lordly" skeleton driver, and its "select" party of skeleton "professional beauties" on top. It made quite a white glare as it passed in the sickly sun, and scattered a good deal of bone-dust from its wheels. Quite close to me there were a couple of skeletons engaged in love dallyings of the most ethereal description. The one, a female, was seated in a victoria, sheltering the top of her skull (on which a fashionable bonnet was perched) with a black lace parasol lined in crimson—a tint which flung a rouge-like reflection on her fleshless but still sensually-shaped jaws. The other, a man, clothed in "afternoon visiting" costume, leaned tenderly towards her over the park-railing, proffering for her acceptance a spray of white lilies which he had taken from his button-hole, and which he held affectionately between his dry bone fingers. Anything more sublimely chaste, yet "realistic," can never be imagined. The way their two skulls nodded and grinned at each other was intensely edifying—it was a case of purely "spiritual" love and platonic desire, in which the wicked flesh had no existing part. And one of the most remarkable features of the whole pageant was the intense stillness which pervaded the movements of the elegant bony throng of "rank, beauty, and fashion." Not a leaf on the trees rustled, not a joint in any distinguished skeleton cracked. Two skeleton policemen kept order, and the crowd itself kept silence. The skeleton horses rubbed against each other in the press, but not a bone clattered, and not a wheel grated. As noiselessly as mist or rolling cloud, the white-ribbed, motley-clothed multitude moved on; the foot-passengers were skeletons also, and 'Arry, turning empty eye-sockets about, looked quite as "noble" as my lord the duke in his barouche, somewhat more so in fact, though wearing shabbier clothes. A delightful equality ruled the scene—a true "fraternity," fulfilling some of the socialistic ideas to the letter. For once the "row" had cast off hypocrisy, and appeared in its absolutely real aspect—everybody had found out everybody else—there was no polite lie possible; frank Bones declared themselves as Bones, and nothing more. Moreover, each skeleton was so like its neighbour skeleton that there were really no differences left to argue about. The famous beauty,

Lady N., could no longer scowl at her rival, the Duchess of L., because they looked precisely similar, save for a trifling difference in length of jaw, and also for the more impressive fact that one wore blue and the other grey. The bones were the same in each "fair" composition, and as bones, the two ladies were, or seemed to be, amiable enough—it was only the wretched flesh that had made them quarrelsome. And of all things, the chief thing that was truly beautiful to witness was the universal smile that beamed through the vast assemblage. Never had the "row" presented itself to broad daylight with such a sincerely unaffected, all-pervading Grin! From end to end the grin prevailed— horses, dogs, and men—there was not one serious exception. Into the air, into the very sky, the wide, perpetual, toothy smile appeared to stretch itself out illimitably, everlastingly: like a grim satire carved in letters of white bone, it seemed to inscribe itself upon the blue of heaven; a mockery, a savagery, a protest, a curse, and a sneer in one, it spread itself in ghastly dumb mirth to the very edge of the far horizon, till I, watching it, could stand the death's-head jollity no longer. Starting in my chair, I uttered a smothered cry, and awoke. A friendly hand fell on my shoulder—a pair of friendly eyes twinkled good-humouredly into mine. "Hullo! Were you asleep?" And there beside me stood Labby—the genial Labby—with "Truth" glittering all over him. Should I tell him of my queer vision, I thought, as I took his arm and strolled away in his ever-delightful company? No. Why should I bother him with the question of honest Bones *versus* dishonest Flesh? He was (and is) already too busy exposing Shams.

V

How Names are Superior to Persons

W hat's in a name?" sighed the fair Juliet of Shakespeare's fancy. She was very much in love when she propounded the question, so she must be excused for coming to the conclusion that a name meant nothing. But no one who is not in love, no one who is not absolutely mad, can be pardoned for indulging in such an opinion. Romeo was more than his name to Juliet, but out of romantic poesy, nobody is more than his name as a rule. The Name is everything; the Person behind the Name is generally nothing when you come to know him. A fine title frequently covers the most unpretentious individual. Beginning with the very highest example in the land, can there be anything more lofty-sounding than this—"Her Majesty Victoria Regina, Queen of Great Britain and Ireland, and Empress of India!" The full-mouthed, luscious, trumpet-roll of this description calls up before the imagination something beyond all speech to express; visions of great nations, glittering armies, stately war-ships, kingdoms of the Orient, stores of wealth and wonder untold—well, and after it all, when you come to stand face to face with this so tremendous Victoria Regina, you find only a dear, simple old lady attired in dowdy black, who might just as well be Mrs. Anybody as the Queen, for all she looks to the contrary. She is a dreadful disappointment to the young and enthusiastic, who almost expect to see something of the enthroned goddess about her, with Athene's shield and buckler bracing her woman's breast, and all the jewels of her Eastern Empire blazing on her brow. Alas for the young and enthusiastic! They are doomed to a great many such disillusions. They dream of Names, and find only Persons, and the fall from their empyrean is an almost paralysing shock as a rule. There are exceptions of course. There is a majestic Cardinal in Rome who looks every inch a Cardinal—the others might be anybodies or nobodies. The Pope is not entirely disappointing; he has the air of a refined Spanish Inquisitor, a sort of etherialised Torquemada. He is much more impressive in demeanour than our own excellent Archbishop of Canterbury, who does not overawe us at any time. In fact, we are seldom awed by persons at all, only by names. A small boy of my acquaintance, taken to see the Shah, expressed his disgust in a loud voice—"Why, he's only a man!" There is the whole mischief of the thing. Only a man—only a woman. Nothing more. But the Names seem so much more. Names spread themselves in a large, vast way over the habitable globe—they are everywhere, while the Persons remain limited to one place, or else are nowhere. The name of Shakespeare is so all-pervading that we will not hear of Bacon being substituted for it, even though Donelly should chance to be right. How well it is for us that we never knew the Person (whoever he was) that wrote the plays. Even Homer himself—should we have cared to know him? I doubt it. His name has proved infinitely better than himself because more lasting. And so, what slight amount of reverence I have in my nature I bestow entirely on Names—for Persons I have little or no respect. A great name possesses a great charm—a great person is generally a great bore. Any one who takes the trouble to observe society closely will support my theory of the superiority of names to individuals. Try the mere sound of several names and see. "The Prince of Wales." That is a fine historical designation, but, curiously enough, it does not convey so much in the way of grand suggestions as it ought to do. Yet he who bears it now is the first gentleman in the land; kindly, courteous, chivalrous, and a veritable Prince of good fellows. "Baron Rothschild"—a name suggestive of wealth galore—but the great financier himself is not such wondrous company. "His Grace the Duke of Marlborough" hath a pleasing roll in the utterance, but when you get close to the distinguished biped so designated, you are conscious of a dismal sense of failure somewhere. "Her Grace the Duchess of Torrie MacTavish" suggests a "gathering of the clans" and bonfires on the Highland hills, but her Grace herself is but a little mean old Scotchwoman, with an avaricious eye upon every "bawbee" expended in her household. "Prime Minister" is a fine title—"Prime Minister of England"—the finest title in the world; but Salisbury is the only man who looks the stately part. The G.O.M. is pure Plebeian—a big-brained plebeian, if you like, but plebeian to the marrow. The demagogue declares itself in the shape of his feet and hands, which are as long and flat as it is the privilege of demagogue hands and feet to be. Coming to the "dream-weavers," or men of letters, some of us (young and enthusiastic) breathe the name "Tennyson" with reverential tenderness, thinking the old man must be well-nigh a demi-god. Not a bit of it. Crusty and perverse, he will have little of our company, and against many of those who have bought his books he thunders denunciation and bars his garden-gate. A little of the exquisite vanity of old Victor Hugo, who used to show himself to passers-by at his window, would better become our veteran Laureate than his hermit-like sourness. "Ruskin" is another great name—but who can count the intense disappointments entailed on ardent admirers of the Name when they discover the Person! "Swinburne" suggests poetry, romance, wild and wondrous things—a bitter awakening awaits those who will insist on peering behind the Name to see the bearer thereof. And it is nearly always so. Names open to us the gates of the Ideal—Persons shut us up in the dungeon of Commonplace. Few famous people come up to their names—still fewer go beyond them. If ever I chance to meet a celebrated man or woman whose personal charm fascinates me more than his or her celebrated name, I shall make a great fuss about it. I shall—let me see, what shall I do?—why, I shall write to the *Times*. The *Times* is the only correct threepenny outlet for ebullitions of sincere national feeling. But till I am otherwise convinced, I adhere to my expressed opinion that Names are the chief motors of social influence, and that individuals are of infinitely less account. Thus, I think it a thousand pities that Stanley did not meet with the good old style of melo-dramatic hero's death in the Dark Continent. His Name might have become a glory and a watchword—as matters now stand his Person has extinguished his Name.

Yes, my dear friends all, I assure you, on my honour as an honest masquer, that both my opinion and advice in this matter are well worth following. When you have selected a Name to hold in some particular reverence, you will be unwise if you try to peep behind it in search of the person belonging to it. The Name is like the door forbidden to Bluebeard's wife: once opened, it shows no end of horrors, headless corpses of good intentions weltering in their blood, and hacked limbs of fine sentiment mouldering on the floor. Keep the door shut therefore. Never unlock it. Let no light fall through the crannies. Stand outside and worship what you imagine may be within. Do as I do—know as many Names as you like and as few Persons as possible. Life is more agreeable that way. For example, if you wanted to find *me* out, and you were to peep behind my name and tear off my domino, you would only be disappointed. You would find nothing but—a person; a Person who might possibly be your friend and might equally be your foe. 'Twere well to be wary in such a doubtful business. Best accept me as I appear, and entertain yourselves with the notion that there may be a "Somebody" hidden behind the mask. Make an "ideal" of me if you choose—ideal saint, or devil, whichever pleases your fancy, for I have no taste either way. Only, for Heaven's sake, remember that if you do persuade yourselves into thinking I am a Somebody, and I turn out after all to be a Nobody, it is not my fault. Don't blame me; blame your own self-deception. Inasmuch as it is especially necessary in my case to bear in mind that the Name is not the Person.

VI

Converseth with Lord Salisbury

Excellent and courteous friend, one moment, I beseech you! I know how busy you are, but I also know, much to my satisfaction, that, like a true diplomat and wise man, you give ear to all, even to fools occasionally, inasmuch as from fools sometimes emanate certain snatches of wisdom. Therefore pause beside me for an instant with the patient grace and friendliness I am accustomed to from you; for though I call myself a fool with the heartiest good will, you have often thought and spoken of me otherwise, for which condescension I thank you. It is something to have won your good opinion, inasmuch as you are guiltless of "booming" second-rate literature, in the style of the venerable Woodcutter of Hawarden, for the sake of bringing yourself into notice. Indeed, I think the admirable qualities of your head and heart have hardly been sufficiently insisted upon by the party you serve. And the genius of patriotism and love of Queen and country which inspire your spirit—are these rightly, fairly, acknowledged? No. But what can you or any one else expect from the weak, vacillating souls you are called upon to lead, such as Randolph Churchill, for example, whose political career is but a disappointment and mockery to public onlookers. I consider that you fight single-handed. Your endeavours are noble and fearless, but those who should support you are for the most part cowards—and not only cowards, but selfish cowards; for to some of your party whom I know, a matter of digestion is more paramount than the good of the country. When a leading Conservative finds himself slightly bilious through over-eating, he hastens away abroad, there to nurse his miserable physical ills and pamper his worthless carcase, regardless of, or indifferent to, the fact that, by virtue of his position, if not his brains, his presence in England might be useful and valuable. There are numerous such lazy hounds in your party, my dear Lord, who deserve to be lashed with the whip of a Fox's or a Pitt's eloquence. And I have wondered oft why you have not spoken the lurking reproach against them, the indignant "Shame on you all!" that must have frequently burned for utterance in your mind.

And "shame on you all!" is the cry that leaps to the lips of every true Briton who thinks of the former historical glories of his country, and at the same time observes the lamentable unsteadiness, the lack of courage, the dearth of principle in politicians of every grade to-day. Parliament gabbles; it does not speak. Often it resembles a cackling chorus of old women striving to describe their own and their friends' various ailments. Why is Radicalism rampant? Why is there any Radicalism? Because so many Radicals are honest, hard-working men—honest in their opinions, honest in the utterance of those opinions, honest in thinking that their cause is good. And you, my dear Lord, have a certain sympathy with this active, energetic, vital, if wrong-headed honesty—you know you have. You love your Sovereign, you love your country, you love the constitution, but for all that you cannot but sympathise with integrity. You know that the Monarch has left England pretty much to itself for the last thirty years, and that she has allowed the people to realise that they can get on without her, seeing she will take no part with them in their daily round. A pity! but the evil is done, and it is too late to remedy it. There is practically no social ruler of the realm, and you must confess, good Salisbury, that this fact makes your work difficult. The mass of the people can only be got to understand a monarch who behaves like one, and the more intellectual food you put into them, the more obstinate they become on the point. With similar pigheadedness they can only understand the personality of a prince whose conduct is a princely example; they are quite sure about themselves here, and have the most appallingly distinct notions concerning right and wrong. They do not go to church for these notions—no. Many cobblers and coalheavers would be mentally refreshed if they were allowed to kick a few seeming-holy clerics whose hypocrisies are apparent despite sermons on Sunday. It must not be forgotten that education is making huge strides among the populace; it has got its seven-leagued boots on, and is clearing all manner of difficulties at a bound. When your greengrocer studies Plato o' nights, when your shoemaker carries the maxims of Marcus Aurelius about in his pocket to refresh himself withal in the intervals of stitching leather, when the wife of your butcher sheds womanly tears over Keats' "Pot of Basil," a poem which the "cultured" dame has "no time" to read—these be the small signs and tokens of a wondrous change by and by. Cheap literature, especially when it is a selection of the finest in the world, is a dangerous "factor" in the making of revolutions, and among other purveyors of literary food for the million, one who calleth himself

Walter Scott, of Newcastle-on-Tyne, is unconsciously doing a curious piece of work. He is putting into the hands of the "lower classes," for the moderate price of one shilling (discount price ninepence) small volumes well bound and well printed, which contain the grandest thoughts of humanity, such as "Epictetus," "Seneca," Mazzini's "Essays," "Sartor Resartus," "Past and Present," the "Religio Medici," the Emerson "Essays," and what not—and it is necessary to take into consideration the fact that the people who buy these books read them. Yes, they read them, every line, no matter how slowly or laboriously; for whether they have expended a shilling or the discount ninepence, they always want to know what they have got for their money. This is the peculiar disposition of the "masses"; the "upper ten" are not so particular, and will lay out a few guineas on Mudie by way of annual subscription, getting scarce anything back of value in exchange. After this fashion, too, the "upper ten" entertain the ungrateful, keep horses and carriages for display, and trot the dreary round of season after season, striving to extract amusement from the dried-up gourd of modern social life, and finding nothing in it all but a bitter jest or a sneering laugh at the slips in morality of their so-called "friends" and neighbours. And thus it is, my dear Lord, that the balance of things is becoming alarmingly unequal; the "aristocratic" set are a scandal to the world with their divorce cases, their bankruptcies, their laxity of principle, their listless indifference to consequences; they never read, they never learn, they never appear to see anything beyond themselves. Whereas the "bas-peuple" *are* reading, and reading the books that have helped to make national destinies— they *are* learning, and they are not afraid to express opinions. They do not think a duke who seduces his friend's wife merely "unfortunate"— they call him in plain language a low blackguard. They cannot be brought to believe that the heir to a great name who has gambled away all his estates on the turf a "gentleman"—they call him a "loose fish" without parley. Now you, excellent and true-hearted Salisbury, have to look on two sides of the question. On the one are your own people, the aristocrats, the Tories, lazy, indifferent, inert, many of them—fond of what they term "pleasure," and as careless of the interests of the country (with a few rare exceptions) as they can well be. On the other hand you have the sturdy, loyal, splendid English "masses," who in their heart of hearts are neither Radicals, Whigs, or Tories, but are simply as they always have been—"For God and the Right!" It matters not which party expresses what they consider the Right; it is the Right they want, and the Right they will have, and they will try all means and appliances in their power till they get it. And it is with this clamour for the Right that you, my Lord, sympathise, because you know how much there is just now that is wrong; how politicians shuffle and lie and play at cross-purposes simply to attain their own personal ends; how over-competition is cutting the throat of Free Trade; how foolishly the tricksters have played with poor distracted Ireland; how openly we have lowered the standard of society by admitting into it men and women of well-known degraded reputation, as well as the painted mimes and puppets of the stage; how wives are bargained for and bought for a price, almost as shamelessly as in an open market; how good faith, chivalry, honour, and modesty are every day becoming rarer and rarer among men; and how, worst of all, we try to cover our vices by a cloak of hypocrisy—the most canting hypocrisy current in the world. English hypocrisy, the ultra-pious form—oh! "it is rank; it smells to heaven!" There is nothing like it anywhere—nothing—no devil so well sainted by psalm-singing, church-going, Sunday observance, and charitable subscription lists. The married woman of title and high degree who sells the jewel of her wifely chastity for the trifling price of a fool's praise, is ever careful to look after the poor, and give her "distinguished" patronage to church-bazaars. Pah! such things are as a sickness to the mind; one's gorge rises at them; and yet they are, as the Queen said to Hamlet, "common." So common, i' faith, that we are beginning to accept them as an inevitable part of our "social observances." And, alas, my Lord of Salisbury, you can do nothing to remedy these things, and yet it is precisely "these things" that swell the rising wave of Radicalism. And despite all the power of your keen, capacious brain, and all the love of country working in your soul, believe me, the storm will break. Nothing will keep it back; because, though there are men of genius in the realm, these men are not permitted to speak. The tyrant Journalism forbids. Why "tyrant"? Is not Journalism free? Not so, my Lord; it is not the "voice of the people" at all; it is simply the voice of a few editors. Were the most gifted man that ever held a pen to write a letter to any of the papers on a crying subject of national shame, he would be refused a hearing unless he were a friend of the proprietors of whatever journal he elected to write to. And men of genius seldom are friends of editors—a curious fact, but true. And so we never really hear the "voice of the people" save in some great crisis, and when we do, it invariably astonishes us. It upsets our nerves, too, for a long time afterwards. It is always so horribly loud, authoritative and convincing! The "voices of editors" die away on these occasions like the alarmed squealings of cats chased by infuriated hounds, and into the place of such a smug and well-satisfied person as the Editor of the *Times*, for example, leaps a shabby, dirty, hungry, eager-eyed creature like Jean Jacques Rousseau, who, instead of a clean and carefully prepared pen, uses for the nonce a red, sputtering torch of revolution, which, setting fire to old abuses, spreads wide conflagration through the land. And how the heart leaps, how the blood thrills, when old abuses *are* destroyed! When the rats' nests of cliques are thrust out to perish in the gutter, when the dirty cobwebs of self-interest and love of gain are swept down, and the fat spiders within them trampled under foot, when the great white palace of national Honour is cleansed and made sweet and fresh for habitation, even at the cost of groaning labour, confusion, and stress, how one breathes again, how one lives the life of a true man in the purified strong air!

As you know well, my Lord, I am of no political party. I am proud to be as one with this great nation in its vital desire for the Right and the Just. Wherever the Right appears I am its follower to the death. I hate false things; I hate bubble reputations, empty wind-bags of policy, dried skeletons of faith. Why not leave this dubious handling of bones and dusty material? It is too late to set wry matters straight. They are an obstruction, and must be cleared from the path of England. Had you the temerity, as I know you have the will, you would speak your thoughts more openly than you have yet done. You would say: "I refuse to lead cowards. I will call to my side men of proved brain and honesty and skill, with whom honour is more than pelf; I will get at the heart of England, and move with *its* pulsations; and of those who are not with this heart I will have none. I will at once make some attempt to remedy the frightful abuses of the law; I will move heaven and earth till England, not party, is satisfied!"

And oh, my most excellent friend, what a wise thing you would do, if you would only keep a watchful eye on the scribblers—the poor and hungry and ambitious scribblers especially! Your party at all times of history has been foolishly prone to neglect this sort of inky folk, and what an error of policy is such neglect! These same inky folk, my Lord, do cause thrones to fall and empires to tremble, wherefore you and all whom it concerns should look after them warily. Make friends with them; soothe their irritated nerves; take time and trouble to explain a situation to them, and remember, never was there dusty, crusty writing-biped yet but could not be moved to a pale, pleased smile of response to a royal hand-shake, a royal greeting, given in good season. It is not singers and twiddlers on musical strings that a wise Court should patronise, but the wielders of pens—they, who, if despised and neglected, take relentless vengeance, and, fearing neither God nor devil, proceed to make strange bargains with both. The Press is a plebeian creature—yes, I know; but for all that, it has stumbled with its big, hob-nailed shoes and Argus eyes into the Royal precincts, and stands there smacking its greasy lips and staring rudely, after the fashion of all plebeians unaccustomed to polite society. It is vulgar, this Press—there is no doubt of that; it dresses badly, and wears, not a sword by its side, but a stumpy pen stuck unbecomingly behind its ear, and it gives itself a vast amount of coarse swagger because it is for the most part deficient in education, and picks up its knowledge by hearsay—nevertheless it has power. And it is a power which neither you nor any one else can afford to despise; wherefore, good friend, when you have any grand object in view and want to attain it, let all else go if necessary, but gather a grand muster-roll of Pens. These shall win you your cause if you only know how to lead them, and without their assistance you shall be lost in a sea of contradictions. Some of these Pens are already yours to command; but others are not, and you trouble not your head concerning these "others" which are the very ones you should secure. As for me, I could go on advising you with the most infinite tedium on sundry matters, but I will not now, inasmuch as we shall have frequent opportunities for discourse in the library at Hatfield. And so, till we meet again, accept the assurance of my admiration and devoted service. You are one of the noblest of living Englishmen; you have the kindest heart in the world; your foreign policy means peace and satisfaction to Europe; and yet, with it all, and with my ardent friendship for you, I cannot help asking myself the question whether, if the storm breaks and the waves rise mountains high, will you have the strength to be a pilot for the ship of England in her dark hour? And if it should be proved that you cannot steer us, Who shall be found that can?

VII

Chatteth with the Grand Old Man

Dost thou remember, my dear Mr. Gladstone, a certain warm and pleasant July afternoon when thou didst honour and oppress me with thy Grand Old Presence for a couple or more of weary hours, regardless of the fact that the "House" expected thee to appear and reply on some moot point or other to Mr. Goschen? There in my modest studio thou didst sit, rubbing that extensive ear of thine with one long forefinger, and smiling suavely at such regular intervals as almost to suggest the idea of there being a patent smiling-machine secreted behind thy never-resting jaw!

Ah, that was a day! We talked—but no! 'twas thou didst talk, thou noble old man! and I—as all poor mortals must needs do in thy company—listened. Listened intently; helpless to remove thee from the chair in which thou sattest; hopeless of putting any stop to thine eloquence; while on, on, on, still on, rolled the stream of thy fluent and wordy contradictions, till my mind like a ship broken loose from its moorings, rocked up and down in a wild, dark sea of uncertainty as to what thou didst mean; or whether thy meaning, if it could by chance be discovered, should in truth be meant? Hadst thou been a Book instead of a Man, I should have flung thee aside, walked the room, and clutched my hair after the manner of the intense tragedian; but with thee, thou astonishing Biped, I could do no more than stare stonily at thy careless collar-ends and concentrate all my soul on my powers of hearing. "Listen, fool!" I said to my inner self—"Listen! It is Gladstone who is speaking—Gladstone the old man eloquent; Gladstone the thinker; Gladstone the Bible scholar; Gladstone the Greek translator; Gladstone the Scotchman, Gladstone the Irishman, Gladstone the—the—the—Wood-cutter! Listen!"

And, as I live, I listened to thee, Gladstone; I swallowed, as it were, thine every word, in spite of increasingly lethargic mental indigestion. Specially did I strive to follow thee in thy wild flights up the stairs of many religious theories, when with gray hair ruffled and eyes aglare, thou didst solemnly rend piecemeal "Robert Elsmere," forgetting, O thou grand old Paradox, that if thou hadst never lifted up that clamant voice of thine in *Nineteenth-Century-Magazine* utterance, Robert and his oppressive religious troubles might scarcely have attracted notice? Didst thou not "boom" Robert, and then feign surprise at the result? Ay, venerable Splitter of Straws and Hewer of Logs, wilt deny the truth? And shall I not advise thee in thine own terms to retire from public life, not "now," but "at present." Or if not "at present" then "now"? Either will serve, before thou dost make more blows with thy hatchet-brain (somewhat dulled at the edge) at the future honour and welfare of thy country.

Ah, what things I could have said to thee, thou Quibble, when thou didst venture to assail me with thy converse, if thou hadst but taken decent pause for breathing! Why, amongst other marvels, didst thou deem it worth thy while to flatter me, or to praise the casual sputterings of my pen? Thy unctuous insinuations carried no persuasion; thy "nods and becks and wreathed smiles" were wasted on me; thy soft assurances of the "certainty of my future brilliant fame" went past my ears like the murmur of an idle wind. For a fame "assured" by thee is nothing worth; and thy Polonius-like approbation of any piece of work, literary or otherwise, is as a mark set on it to make it seem ridiculous. For thou art destitute of humour save in wood-cutting; and thou needest many a lesson from my dear friend Andrew Lang before thou canst successfully comprehend the subtly critical art of proving a goose to be a swan. And so, by monosyllables slipt in like frailest wedges between thy florid bursts of ambiguity, I strove to entice thy wandering wits back to the discussion of personal faith in matters religious, wherein I found thee most divertingly inchoate, but my feeble efforts were of small avail. For lo, while yet I strove to understand whether thou wert in truth a Roman Papist, a Calvinist, a Hindoo, a Theosophist, or a Special Advocate of the *War Cry*, the subject of Creed, like a magic-lantern slide, disappeared from thy mental view, and Divorce came up instead. Frightful and wonderful, according to thee, goodman Gladstone, are the wicked ways of the married! No sooner are they united than they move heaven and earth to get parted—so it is at any rate very frequently in the free and happy American Republic, where the disagreeing parties need not move heaven and earth, but simply make a mutual assertion. Oh, of a truth here was no smiling matter! No Deity in question, but a very positive Devil, needing thy exhortation and exorcism; and thy jaws clacked on sternly, strenuously, and with a resolute gravity and persistency that seemed admirable. Not every man could be expected to find a Mrs. Gladstone, but surely all were bound to try and discover such a paragon. If all married society were composed of Mr. and Mrs. Gladstones, why, married society would realise the fabled Elysium. And supposing there continued to be only one Mr. and Mrs. Gladstone, and all the rest were quite a different set of hopelessly different temperaments, then, naturally, it was impossible to state what disasters might ensue. It would be a case of Noah and his wife over again—after them the Deluge. In the interim, Divorce was shocking, abominable, sinful, diabolical, ungodly—an upsetting of the most sacred foundations of morality—and it was chiefly because Gladstonian domestic tastes were not universal. This, at least, is what I seemed to gather from thee in thine onslaughts against the large and melancholy mass of the Miserably Married; I say I "seemed" to gather it, because it "seemed" thy meaning, but as thy whole mode of speech and action is only "seems," I cannot be absolutely sure either of myself or thyself. For thou didst set out an attractive row of various learned propositions, gently, and with the bland solicitude of a hen-wife setting out her choicest eggs for sale, then suddenly and incontinently, and as one in a fit of strangest madness, thou didst sweep them up and fling them aside into airy nothingness without concern for the havoc wrought. Thou didst calmly state what appeared to be a Fact, reasonable and graspable; and with all the powers of my being I seized upon it as a grateful thing and good for consideration; when suddenly thy senile smile obscured the intellectual horizon, and thy equally modulated voice murmured such words as these: "Not that I desire to imply by any means that this is so, or should be so, but that it might (under certain circumstances, and provided certain minds were at harmony upon the point) probably become so." Ah, thou embodied Confusion worse Confounded! Had it not been for this constant playing of thine at thy favourite shuffling game of cross-purposes, I should have roused my soul from its stupor of forced attention to demand of thee more of thy profound Bible scholarship. Whether, for example, if Divorce, thy bugbear, were ungodly, and the Bible true, a man should not have two, three, nay, half-a-dozen wives at his pleasure for as long or as short a time as he chose, and find situations for them afterwards as servants, telegraph-clerks, and bookkeepers, when their beauty was gone and snappishness of temper had taken the place of endearing docility. Whether English harem-life, lately set in vogue by certain great and distinguished "Upper" people, could not be easily proved pleasing unto the Most High Jehovah? For did not God love His servant Abraham? and did not Abraham bestow his affections on Sarai and Hagar? and when the hoary old reprobate was "well stricken in years" and "the Lord had blessed him in all things" did he not again take a wife named Keturah, who presented him in his centenarian decrepitude with six sons?—all "fine babies," no doubt. What sayest thou to these morals of Holy Writ, thou "many-sounding" mouthpiece of opinion? Answer me on a postcard, for with thee, more than with any other man, should brevity be the soul of wit!

Some of us younger and irreverent folk oft take to speculating why, in the name of bodies politic, thy days, O Venerable, are so long in the land which the Lord thy God giveth thee? The Lord thy God, friend William Ewart, must have some excellent reason for allowing thee to ruthlessly cut down so many growing oaks of English honour and walk unscathed across the bare, disfigured country, with the wild dogs of Democracy sneaking at thy heels. And I forgot, in speaking of the holy Abraham, that late events have proved the high superiority of thy tastes in morality to those of God's anciently-favoured servant. For didst thou not disown thy sweetest nursling, thine own favourite adopted son, Parnell, simply and solely to publicly clasp and kiss the wrinkled, withering hand of Mrs. Grundy? And knowest thou not, thou gray-haired Conundrum, that nothing has ever seemed more preternaturally absurd to the impartial observer and student of social life in all countries, than this making a public question out of personal matter?—this desertion of a former friend, a man, too, of immense intellectual capability, all because, as the old German ballad goes, "he loved a, to him, temptingly-forbidden lady"? Just Heavens! I could name dozens of men (but I will not), party men too, respectably married likewise, who have their "temptingly-forbidden ladies" tucked snugly away in the innermost recesses of their confidence, and who avoid betraying themselves into such impulsiveness as might lead to a fire-escape and political dissolution. As for Mrs. Grundy, the dear old soul never sees anything now unless she is led up to it with her spectacles on; she is more than half blind, and totally deaf—a poor, frail creature very much on her last legs—and she must have been vaguely flattered and surprised at thy voluntary Grand Old Hand-Shake, given to her in the very face of all the staring world of intelligence and fashion. It must have soothed her aching heart and comforted her tottering limbs to find she still had left to her a pale vestige of past power. Ah, it was a grand and edifying party-split!—almost as exciting as if it had occurred on a question of Beer, which fateful subject angrily discussed, did, I believe, on one occasion actually effect a change of Ministry. And it is rather a notable proof of the curious littleness of the age we live in, that of late, political parties have seldom broken up on great questions—questions of momentous and general interest affecting the welfare of the state and people—but nearly always on petty, personal, nay almost vulgar and childish disputes, such as might make Fox and Pitt turn and groan in their graves. Is there no such thing as unadulterated patriotism left, I wonder?—no real ardent love of the "Mother" England? or hast thou, old Would-Be Despot, choked it all by thy pernicious gabble?

And yet, whatever may be said of thee now or in after history as a Man-Enigma, thy bitterest enemy, unless he be an idiot born, can hardly be blind to thy numerous and extraordinary endowments. Jumbled as they are together with so much confusion that it is difficult to tell which savour most of vice or most of virtue, they are nevertheless Endowments, rare enough to find in any other living composition of mortal mould. And the mystic gift that keeps thee powerful to grasp and retain thy dominance over the minds of the Majority, is simple Genius—a gift of which there are many spurious imitations, but which in itself is given to so few as to make it seem curious and remarkable, aye, even a thing suggestive of downright madness to the men of mere business talent and capacity who form the largest portion of the governing body. Misguided, captious, flighty as caprice itself, it is nevertheless a flash of the veritable Promethean fire which works that busy, massive brain of thine—a kindling, restless heat which is entirely deficient in the brains of nearly all thy fellow-statesmen of the hour. This it is that fascinates the Public—the giant Public that above all the whisperings and squealings of the Press, reserves its own opinion, and only utters it when called upon to do so, with sundry roarings and vociferations as of a hungry lion roused—a convincing manner of eloquence which doth wake to speculative timorousness the wandering penny-a-liner. For Genius is the only quality the Public does in absolute truth admire, without being taught or forced into admiration—and that Genius has ever in reality been despised or neglected by the world, is, roughly speaking, a Lie. Everything noble that deserves to live, lives; and Homer wrote as much for the England of to-day as for the Greece of past time. The things that die, deserve to die; the "genius" who deems himself ill-used, does by his childish querulousness prove himself unworthy of appreciation. For no great soul complains, inasmuch as all complaint is cowardice.

Thus, when I bring the Public well into sympathetic view, and consider thee in relation to it, O Grand Old Gladstone, I understand readily enough what is meant by the feeling of the "majority" concerning thy civic and personal qualifications for power. It is this—that the people feel, that notwithstanding thy chameleon-like variableness, and thy darkly cabalistic utterances on the political How, When, and Why, thou art still the "only" man in the professed service of the country possessing this talisman of Genius which from time immemorial has carried its own peculiar triumph over the heads of all opposers. For when thou shalt be gone the way of all flesh, who is left? Little brilliancy of wit or good counsel is there now in the Commons, and the Lords are but weary creatures, bent on maintaining their own interests in the face of all change. Is there a man who can be truly said to have the gift of eloquence save Thou? Wherefore the attention and interest of the people still continue to revolve round thy charmed pivot, thou Hawarden Thinker, with, as the Scotch say, "a bee" in thy bonnet. And, whether Premier or Ex-Premier, all because thou *art* a Thinker in spite of the bee. Thy thoughts may be "long, long thoughts" like the "thoughts of youth" in Longfellow's pretty poem—they may be indeed without any definite end at all, but they are thoughts, they are not mere business calculations of the State's expenses. Only being ill-assorted and still worse defined, they are unfit to blossom into words, which they generally do, to the perplexity and anxiety of everybody concerned. And there is the mischief—a mischief irremediable, for nothing will stop thy tongue, thou Grand Old Gabbler, save a certain Grand Old Silence wearing only bones and carrying a scythe, who is not so much interested in politics as in mould and earthworms *à la* Darwin.

Nevertheless I, for one, shall be exceedingly sorry when this fleshless "reaper whose name is Death" mows thee down, poor Gladdy, and turns thee remorselessly into one more pinch of dust for his overflowing granary. Remember me or not as thou mayest, do me good service or bad, I care nothing either way. Thy visits to me were of thine own seeking, and of conversation thou didst keep the absolute monopoly; but what matter?—I at least was privileged to gaze upon thee freely and mentally comment upon thy collar unreproved. 'Twas but thy unctuous flattery that vexed my soul; for Gladstonian praise is but Art's rebuke. Otherwise I bear thee no malice, though for sundry reasons I might well do so. . . Oh, venerable Twaddler! Didst thou but know me as I am, would not the hairs upon thy scalp, aye "each particular hair" rise one by one in anger and astonishment, and thou for once be rendered speechless? . . . Nay, good Gladstone-Grundy, have no fear! I will not blab upon thee; I am well covered, closely masked; and thou shalt hear no more of me as I slip by, save. . . a smothered laugh behind my domino!

VIII

Of the True Journalist and His Creed

I am very fond of journalists. I look upon them, young and old, fat and lean, masculine and feminine, as the salt of the earth wherewith to savour the marrow of the country. And I like to put them through their paces. I am always devoured by an insatiable curiosity to fathom the depths of their learning—depths which I feel are almost infinite; yet despite this infinity I am always fain to plunge. Whenever I see a son of the ink-pot I collar him, and demand of him information—information on all things little and big, because he knows all things. I believe he even knows why Shakespeare left his second-best bed to his wife, only he won't tell. As for languages, he is everybody's own Ollendorf. He knows French, he knows Russian, he knows Italian, he knows Spanish, he knows Hindustani, he knows Chinese, he knows—oh divine Apollo! what does he *not* know! Let anybody write a book and try to introduce into its pages one word of Cherokee, one wild unpronounceable word, and the omniscient journalist is down upon him instantly with the bland assertion that it is a wrong word, wrongly spelt, wrongly used. For the journalist knows Cherokee; he spoke it when a gurgling infant in his mother's arms, together with all the living and dead dialects of all nations. So that when I get a journalist to dine with me, is it to be wondered at that I am consumed by a desire to *know*? The thirst of wisdom enters into me, and having plied my man with eatables and wine, I hang on his lips entranced. For can he not tell me everything that ever was, or ever shall be?—and shall I not also aspire to oracles?

Once upon a time, to my unspeakable joy, I caught a fledgling journalist; a fluttering creature, all eagle-wings and chuckles, and I carried him home in a cab to dinner. He was a wild fowl, with plumage unkempt, and beak, *i.e.*, a Wellingtonian nose, that spoke volumes of knowledge already. I discovered him hopping about a club, and seeing he was hungry, I managed to coax him along to my "den." When I had him there safe, I could have shouted with pure ecstasy! He became gentle; he smoothed his ruffled feathers; he dipped his beak into my burgundy wine and pronounced in a god-like way that "behold, it was very good." Then, when his inner man was satisfied, he spoke; and information, information, came rolling out with every brief and slangy sentence. Of kings and queens, of princes and commoners, of he and she and we and they, of fire, police, law, council, parliament, and my lady's chamber, of all that whirls in the giddy circle of our time, my fledgling had taken notes—yea, even on the very wheels of government, he had placed his ink-stained finger.

"O wondrous young man!" I muttered as I heard; "O marvel of the age! Why do not the kings of the earth gather together to hear thy wisdom? Why do not the councils of Europe wait to learn the arts of government from thee? Wert thou at the right hand of Deity, I wonder, when worlds were created and comets begotten?" . . . Here, filled with ideas, I poured more wine out for the moistening of the Wellingtonian beak, and demanded feverishly—"Tell me, friend, of things that are unknown to most men—tell me of the dark mysteries of time, which must be clear as daylight to a brain like yours!—instruct me in faith and morals—show me the paths of virtue—explain to me your theories of the future, of creed—"

I stopped, choked by my own emotion; I felt I was on the point of comprehending the incomprehensible—of grasping great facts made clear through the astute perception of this literary Gamaliel. And he arose in response to my adjuration; he expanded his manly chest, and stood in an attitude of "attention"; his nose was redder than when he first sat down to dine, and the vacuous chuckle of his laugh was music to my soul.

"Creed!" said he. "Drop that! I'm not a church-goer. I've got one form of faith though." And he chuckled once again.

"And that is?" I questioned eagerly.

"This!"

And with proud unction he recited the following simple formula:—

I believe in the *Times*.

And in the *Morning Post*, Maker of news fashionable and unfashionable.

And in one *Truth*, the property of one Labby, the only-begotten son of honesty in Journalism,

Who for us men and our salvation, socially, legally, and politically,

Came down from Diplomacy into Bolt Court, Fleet Street,

And was there self-incarnated Destroyer of Shams. Labby of Labby, Truth of Truth, Very Rad of Very Rad, Born not made, Being one with himself and answerable to nobody for his opinions.

Member for Northampton, he suffered there, secured votes and was left unburied,

And he sitteth in the House, save when he ariseth and speaketh,

And he will continue with triumph to judge all those that judge, both the living and the dead,

Whose "legal pillory" shall have no end.

And I believe in one *Pall Mall Gazette*, Pure Giver of frequently mistaken information, which proceedeth from pens feminine,

And which with the soporific *St. James's*, together, exerteth the lungs of the newsboys.

I acknowledge one holy and absolute *Court Circular*.

I confess one "*Saturday*" for the flaying of new authors,

And I look for the death of the *Nineteenth Century*

And the life of a less dull magazine to come Amen.

With this, my journalistic fledgling gave way to Homeric laughter, and helped himself anew to wine. And since that day, since that witching hour, I have watched his wild career. I track him in the magazines; I recognise the ebullitions of his wit in "society" paragraphs; I discover his withering, blistering sarcasm in his reviews of the books he never reads; in fact, I find him everywhere. As the air permeates space, he permeates literature. He is the all-sure, the all-wise, the all-conquering one. With such a faith as his, so firmly held, so nobly uttered, he is born to authority. I only wish some one would make him Prime Minister. Everything that is wrong would be righted, and with a Journalist (and such a journalist!) at the head of affairs, all questions of government would be as easy to settle as child's play. He himself—the Journalist—implies as much, and with all the fibres of my soul I believe him!

IX

Of Writers in Grooves

There are a certain class of authors who remind me of a certain class of gamblers—men who believe in a special "lucky number," and are always staking their largest amounts upon it. To speak more plainly, I should say that I mean the "groovy" men, who, as soon as they find one particular sort of "style" that chances to hit the taste of the public, keep on grinding away at it with the remorselessness of an Italian street-organ player. I see lots of such fellows in the crowd around me, and I know most of them personally. For instance, there is William Black, a distinctly "groovy" man if ever there was one. All his books are like brothers and sisters, bearing a strong family resemblance one to another. If you have read "A Princess of Thule" and "A Daughter of Heth" you have got the *crème de la crème* of all that was or is in him. The rest of his work is evolved from precisely the same substance as is found in these two books, only it is drawn out into various criss-cross threads of deft weaving; and, deft as it is, it makes uncommonly thin material. In his latter novels, indeed, there is so much of what may be justly termed "feminine twaddle," that one has to look back to the title-page in order to convince one's self that it is really one of the "virile" sex who is telling a story. Excellent Willie! With his small head and inoffensive physiognomy, he suggests an intellectual sort of pint-pot, out of which it would be absurd to expect a quart of brain. Inasmuch as a pint-pot can only hold a pint; so let us be grateful for small mercies. And let us admire, not for the first time either, the persistent kindly confidence of the British Public, who steadily take up Willie's novels, one after the other, in the sanguine faith of finding something new therein. "Some day," says the patient B.P. in its trot to and from Mudie's Library—"some day Willie will give us a book without a sunset in it. Some day, by happy chance, he will forget there exists such a thing as a yacht. And some day—who knows?—he may even awaken to the fact that there are other places on earth besides Scotland, and other men who are as interesting as Scotchmen."

Good B.P.! Excellent B.P.! What a heart you have! You deserve the very best that can be given you for the sake of your tolerance and cheerfulness of temper, which qualities in you seem truly inexhaustible. Here followeth an anecdote: A certain flimsy scribbler I wot of, who had just got himself into a loosely-fitting suit of literary armour, and was handling his sword a bit awkwardly, as beginners at warfare are apt to do, said to me one day, with a sort of schoolboy vaunt, "The Public want *trash*!—and trash is what I'll give them!" O wise judge! O learned judge! Out he went with his "trash," his sword poking into everybody's eye, and his armour waggling uncomfortably round him, and lo! the Public "took" his trash and threw it into the gutter, broke his sword for him, gave him back the pieces, and civilly recommended him to look after the loose places in his armour. He went home, did that proud warrior, and sat thinking about what had chanced—it may be he is thinking still.

No, the B.P. don't want "trash"—they want the best of everything—but they have an infinite kindness and patience in waiting for that "best," and carefully looking out for it; and when it truly comes they welcome it with honest enthusiasm. Thus did they welcome and applaud the "Princess of Thule," because they found it good and charming and unique, and ever since that time they have reposed quite a pathetic trust in little Black, hoping against hope that he will give them something else equally good again. Alas for the vanity of all such human wishes! for William is a "groovy" man now, and in his groove he evidently purposes to remain. I remember dining with, him on one occasion, when, in the ordinary way of conversation, I asked him what books he had been reading lately? Oh, what sublime amazement in his rolling eye!

"Read?" he drawled. "I never read. Reading spoils an author's own style."

Haw-haw! Weally! Good B.P., you see how matters stand? Willie's "kail-yairdie," or little plot of garden-ground, is barren; its first crop has been gathered, and no more seed sown by study, so don't expect any other rich harvests, or look for wonders in such work as "Stand fast, Craig Royston!" For even brain-soil wants cultivation, if it is to produce something better than weeds.

Another "groovy" man is William Clark Russell. The waves rule Britannia in his opinion: The sea occupies his inventive faculty to the exclusion of everything else. A pigmy Neptune sits on his bald pate, touching it up with a trident. Sailors' "yarns," sailors' marriages, sailors' shipwrecks—tales of mariners in every sort of painful and pleasant situation—influence his mind and bring it into that "One-idea" condition which is considered by gravely spectacled specialists as a form of cerebral disease. Moreover, his books bristle with sailors' jargon, sailors' slang, sailors' "lingo," which people, who are not sailors and who never intend to be sailors, do not understand and do not want to understand. However, this monomania of his produced one good result—"The Wreck of the Grosvenor." He exhausted his best energies in that book, and having found it a success (as it deserved to be), settled into the Jack Tar line of writing, and became once for all and evermore "groovy." The "Wreck of the Grosvenor" is his "Princess of Thule." He is all there, and there is no more of him anywhere.

At one time I feared, but it was only a passing shudder, that one of the most brilliant novelists we have, Marion Crawford, was drifting in the fatal direction of "groove." When the rather lengthy "Sant' Ilario" came trailing along, after the equally lengthy "Saracinesca," I thought, "Alas! and woe is me! Are we never to hear the last of the beautiful and lovable Astrardente? A noble character, but somewhat too much of her is here." And I was on the verge of uncomfortable doubt for some time, for I had always judged Crawford to be of the true Protean type of genius, capable of touching every string on the literary harp he holds. And I was not mistaken, for "A Cigarette-maker's Romance," that most delicate and delightful work, proves that he is anything but "groovy"; and his "Witch of Prague" is a breaking of entirely new soil. So that the more I read of him, the more I am confirmed in the opinion I have previously ventured to express—namely, that he is our best man-novelist. I use the term "man-novelist" because I know there are women-novelists—ladies whom I should be very sorry to offend by applying the adjective "best" to any member of the viler sex. For I know also that those ladies, if affronted, have curious and unexpected ways of revenging themselves, and though I am masked, my silver domino is hardly proof against the green and glittering eye of a remorseless literary female. So pray you be not wrathful, sweet ladies!—rather join with me in gentle chorus, and say, as you know you must, that the author of "Dr. Isaacs," "A Roman Singer," and "Marzio's Crucifix" is indeed the least "groovy," and therefore the best "man-novelist" living; be kind and condescending thus far, for of women-novelists you shall have a word presently.

Somewhere, once upon a time, I called George Meredith an Eccentricity. I meant him no harm by this phrase or term—I mean none now, when I repeat it. He *is* an Eccentricity—of Genius! Ha!

where are you now, all you commentators and would-be clearers-up of the Mighty Obscure? An Eccentricity—a bit of genius gone mad—an Intellectual Faculty broken loose from the moorings of Common Sense, and therefore a hopelessly obstinate fixture in the "groove" of literary delirium. A Meredithian description of Meredith is found in his story of "One of our Conquerors"—a description there applied to the character of Dudley Sowerby, but fitting Meredith himself exactly. Here it is; "His disordered deeper sentiments were a diver's wreck where an armoured subtermarine, a monstrous puff-ball of man, wandered seriously light in heaviness, trebling his hundred-weights to keep him from dancing like a bladder-block of elastic lumber; thinking occasionally amid the mournful spectacle, of the atmospheric pipe of communication with the world above, whereby he was deafened yet sustained." Of course it is difficult to grasp all this at once—but I seize upon the words, "*a bladder-block of elastic lumber*"—I know, I feel that "*bladder-block*" is Meredith, though I cannot precisely inform myself or others what a "*bladder-block*" in its original sense may mean. But meanings are not expected to be vulgarly apparent on the surface of this "diver's wreck" or new school of prose—you have to search for them; and you must hold fast to whatever "*atmospheric pipe of communication*" you can find, in order to keep up with this "*Monstrous puff-ball of man wandering seriously light in heaviness*." It has been left to George Meredith to tell us about "the internal state of a gentleman who detested intangible metaphor as heartily as the vulgarest of our gobble-gobbets hate it"—and if we would not be considered "*gobble-gobbets*" ourselves, we must strive to be grateful for the light he throws on our intellectual darkness. He is supposed to understand women in and out and all round, so we must take it for granted that a woman can "breathe thunder." It sounds alarming—it is alarming—but if Meredith says it, it must be true. And he does say it. With the calm conviction of one who knows, he assures us that "the lady breathed low thunder." She is a very remarkable person altogether, this "lady," called Mrs. Marsett, and her modes of action are carried on in positive defiance of all natural and physical law. For at one time we are told "her eye-*lids* (not her eyes) mildly sermonised," and on another occasion she actually "caught at her slippery tongue and carolled," quite a feat of *leger de langue*. Again, "her woman's red mouth was shut fast on a fighting underlip." Till I read this, I was fool enough to think that the underlip was part of the mouth, but now I know that the underlip is quite a separate and distinct thing, as it is able to go on "fighting" while the mouth is "shut fast" on it. She does all sorts of curious things with this mouth of hers, does Mrs. Marsett; in one scene of her career it is said that "she blushed, blinked, frowned, *sweetened her lip-lines, bit at the under one*, and passed in a discomposure." Moreover, this strange mouth was given to the utterance of bad language, for with it and her "slippery tongue" Mrs. Marsett said her own name was "Damnable!" and what was still worse, "had the passion to repeat the epithet in shrieks and scratch up male speech for a hatefuller," whatever that may mean. Of course, it is all very grand and mixed and magnificent, if any one chooses to think so; people can work themselves up into an epilepsy of enthusiasm over prose run mad *à la* Meredith, as over poetry gone a-woolgathering *à la* Browning. It is a harmless mania which is confined to the few, and is of a distinctly non-spreading tendency; while those who are not partakers in the craze can look on thereat and be amused thereby—for Meredith is at all times and all seasons both personally and in literature a real entertainment. Whether he be haranguing to the verge of deafness some stray acquaintance in the Garrick Club; whether he be met, a greybeard solitary, stalking up the slopes of Box Hill, at the foot of which he resides; whether he be inveighing against the "porkers," *i.e.*, the Public, within the precincts of a certain small and extortionate but rigidly pious bookseller's shop in the town of Dorking; or whether he be visited in his own small literary "châlet," which he built for himself in his own garden, away from his house, what time he had a wife, (a very charming, kindly lady, whose appreciative sense of humour enabled her to understand her husband's gifts better than any of his wildest worshippers), in order to escape from "domesticity" and the ways of the "women" he is supposed to understand—in each and all of these positions he is distinctly amusing—and never more so than when he thinks he is impressive. Yet there can be no doubt whatever as to his natural cleverness, and the original turn of mind which might have made him a distinctly great writer, if he had not forced himself into the strained style of the artificial "groove" he has adopted. Even now, if he would only leave the first spontaneous output of his thought alone, instead of altering it when it is on paper, and weighing it down with all the big words he can find in the dictionary, he would probably write something above the average of interest. However, it's no use being hard upon him, as he has quite recently been Lynched. I cannot endure his novels, it is true—but still, I never wished him to meet such a frightful fate. When we reflect on the barbarity of the institution known as Lynch-law, we cannot but wonder how his admirers have tamely stood by and seen him delivered over to so awful a punishment. Yet it is a positive fact that they have made no defence. And he has been torn limb from limb, and broken into explained pieces by a pitiless executioner self-elected to the performance of the abhorrent deed. A woman too—yclept Hannah as well as Lynch; and eke a spinster—mind cannot picture a more formidable foe—a more fearful fate! Heaven save you, poor Meredith! for man cannot. Lynched you are, and Lynched you must be by every word, sentence and chapter, until you be dead, and may God have mercy on your soul!

Among other "groovy" men may be included Hall Caine (whose big "bow-wow" style is utterly unchanged and unchangeable), W. E. Norris, the pale, far-off, feeble imitator of Thackeray, and F. C. Philips. This latter gentleman is evidently fast "set" in the "groove" of naughty but interesting adventuresses. His tale of "As in a Looking-glass" met with so much success, besides receiving the extremely questionable honour of dramatisation, that he now indulges in the error of imagining that all the world must for the future be persistently eager to know the histories of a continuous succession of conscienceless ladies like Lena Despard. One of his creations of the kind, Margaret Byng, might be Lena's twin sister. (According to the title-page, one P. Fendall would seem to have something to do with Margaret Byng, but how and where it is impossible to discover.) Adventuresses for breakfast, adventuresses for dinner, tea and supper; adventuresses in all sorts of gowns, brand-new or shabby, and adventuresses in all sorts of difficult situations at all sorts of seasons—this is the "four-and-twenty blackbirds baked in a pie" kind of dish, which is what we must expect from Mr. Philips in the future. This and no more, since he considers it enough. And among "groovy" men, alas! must be reckoned one of the most delightful of writers, Bret Harte. The "groove" he chose was at first so new and fresh that we all felt as if we could never have enough of it; but even in excess of love there is satiety, and such satiety is our sad experience with the gifted author of "The Luck of Roaring Camp" and the pathetic "Outcasts of Poker Flat." We know exactly the sort of thing he will write for us now—and the charm is broken.

I lay no claim to being possessed of any literary taste, so it will matter to no one when I say I can see no beauty and no art in Mr. Hardy's "Tess of the D'urbervilles." It is an entirely hateful book in my opinion. Neither can I endure Mrs. Ward's "David Grieve," and as this lady has undoubted literary gifts, I hope she will for the future avoid the religious "groove." It is extremely uninteresting, and is enough to cramp any author's style. Mr. Gladstone, who "boomed" "Robert Elsmere," apparently has nothing to say for "David Grieve," though it seems he can admire such crude performances as "Mdlle. Ixe" and "Some Emotions and a Moral." But it would never do for us to go by the taste of the Grand Old Man in these things. He is as variable as a chameleon. He might call our attention to the splendours of Dante on one occasion, and directly afterwards assure us that nothing could be finer in literature than the nursery rhyme of "Pat-a-cake, pat-a-cake, baker's man." Dear old Gladdy! He is the greatest "leader" ever born in his quality of *mis*leading.

It is difficult indeed to find a writer who is not more or less "groovy"—that is, one who will not only give us different stories, but different "styles." And as a rule the men writers are more "groovy" than the women, though the women are bad enough in their own particular way. Miss Braddon, for example, is, as every one knows, the "grooviest" of novelists going—her canvas is always prepared in the same manner, and the same familiar figures stand out upon it in only slightly altered attitudes. Her books always remind me of a child's marionette theatre, having the same set of puppets, who can be placed in position to enact over and over again the same sort of play. And it is a play that always amuses one for an hour, when one has nothing better to do. "Ouida," though she tells all sorts of different stories (of which her short ones are by far the best), has no difference of style—she is always the same old "Ouida"—and so will be to the end of her life's chapter. There are always the same wicked, but exquisitely lovely, ladies, to whom the marriage tie is frailer and less to be considered than a hair, and always the same good, pure, and *therefore* (according to "Ouida") stupid girls who are just sixteen. There are always the bold, bad men with "mighty chests" and "Herculean limbs," who covet their neighbour's wives, or play havoc with the hearts of trusting maidens—and all these things are told with a gorgeousness of colour and picturesqueness of description that is not only brilliant, but very marvellously poetical. "Ouida" holds a pen such as many a man has good secret reason to envy. There are rich suggestions for both poets and painters in many of her books—but there is no convincing portrait of life, except in "Friendship," which was a satirical *exposé* of the actual lives of some very questionable and unpleasant people. Yet "Ouida's" gift was one which might have been turned to rare account had she studied more arduously in her earlier years; but now, across her little garden of genius, in which all the flowers have run wild, are written the fatal words "Too Late."

Another very "groovy" lady novelist is Rhoda Broughton. The not-particularly-good-looking and "loose-jointed" young man (all Miss Broughton's heroes are "loose-jointed"—I don't know why) puts in his appearance in all her books without fail—and there is always the same sort of distressing hitch in the love-business. The liberties she takes with the English language are frequently vulgar and unpardonable. Familiarity with "slang" is no doubt delightful, but some people would prefer a familiarity with grammar.

A very promising creature was the fair American, Amelie Rives. I say "was" because she is married now, and I'm afraid she will not write so well with a "worser half" looking over her "copy." Her story, "Virginia of Virginia," was a delicious study—quite a little work of genius in its way—though I must own her novel, "The Quick or the Dead," was a mere boggle of wild sentiment and scarcely-repressed sensualism. Some critics were very hard down upon her, because she threatened to be "original" all the time, and critics hate that sort of thing. That is why they invariably "go" for one of our newest inflictions, Marie Corelli, of whom it may be truly said that she has written no two books alike, either in plot or style; and the grave *Spectator* on one occasion forgot itself so far as to say that her romance entitled "Ardath" had actually beaten Beckford's renowned "Vathek" out of the field. But all the same, with every respect for the *Spectator's* opinion, I, personally speaking, find her a distinctly exasperating writer, who is neither here, there, nor anywhere—a "will-o'-the-wisp" sort of being, of whom it is devoutly to be wished that she would settle into a "groove," as she would be less of a trial to the (in her case) always savage reviewer.

Nothing is more irritating to a critic than to have to chronicle the reckless flights of this young woman's unbridled and fantastic imagination. She tells us about heaven and hell as if she had been to them both, and had rather enjoyed her experiences. Valiant attempts to "quash" her have been made, but apparently in vain, and most of my brethren in the critical faculty consider her a positive infliction. Why does she not take the advice tendered her by the *World*, and other sensible journals, and retire altogether from literature? I am sure she would be much happier "picking geranium leaves" *à la* Becky Sharp, with a husband and two thousand a-year. As it is, her very name is, to the men of the press, what a red rag is to a bull. They are down upon it instantly with a fury that is almost laughable in its violence. But I suppose she is like the rest of her sex—obstinate, and that she will hold on her wild career, regardless of censure. Only, as I say, I wish she would elect a "groove" to run in, for I, among many others, shall be relieved as well as delighted when we are all quite certain beyond a doubt as to what sort of book we are to expect from her. At present she is a mere vexation to any well-ordered mind.

Poor Mrs. Henry Wood! What a wonderfully "groovy" woman *she* was! always writing, as one of my brother-critics has aptly remarked, "in the style of an educated upper housemaid." And yet her books sell largely—partly because Bentley and Son advertise them perpetually, and partly because they "will not bring a blush to the cheek of the Young Person." This latter reason accounts for the popularity (in the pious provinces) of that astoundingly dull writer, Edna Lyall. Patience almost fails me when I think of that lady's closely-printed, bulky volumes, all about nothing. "Groove"? ye gods! I should think it *was* a "groove"—a religious, goody-goody "groove," out of which there is never the smallest possibility of an escape. But perhaps one of the circumstances that surprises me most in the fate of all the mass of fiction produced weekly, is the curious placidity with which the public take it up, scan it, lay it aside, and forget it instantly. Scarce one out of all the writers writing, male and female, has a book remembered by Mudie's supporters after a year. If any novel is still thought of and talked of after that period, you may be sure it is not "groovy," but that it runs in a directly contrary current to all "grooves" of preconceived opinion—that it has something vaguely irritating about it as well as pleasing—hence its success. But on the whole I am not sure that I do not prefer "groovy" writers after all. There is a comfortable certainty in their literary manœuvres. They are not going to frighten you by exploding a big fiery bomb of Imagination or Truth (both these things are abhorrent to me) on the reader unawares. It is really quite a weird sensation to take up the latest book by a writer who has the reputation of being able to tell you something different each time, because, of course, you never know what he or she may be at. You may have your very soul racked by painful or pathetic surprises—and why should we have our souls racked? The persistently "original" man may take us to the brink of a hell and force us to look down when we would rather not; he may suddenly exert all his forces to drag our leaden minds after him up to a heaven where we are not quite ready to go. Then, again, he may give us descriptions of human passion such as will make us grow quite hot and anon quite cold with the most curious feelings; what have we done that we should be afflicted with literary ague? No; it is better, it is safer, to have our novelists all arranged in "grooves" or "sets" ready to hand, so that we shall know exactly where to find the chroniclers of rural stories, sporting stories, detective stories, ghost stories, every "male and female after their kind," each in his or her own appointed place. To get a book by an author who is recognised as a manufacturer of "racing novels," and find him breaking out into a strain of sublimated philosophy, would be indeed an alarming circumstance to most readers. Oh, yes, it is better to be "groovy"; sometimes the public get tired and throw you over, but that sort of thing happens more frequently in restless France and Italy than in England. Had I been "groovy" I should have been famous—at least, so I have been told by a lady skilled in the fashionable science of palmistry. But being unable to play the mill-horse, and go round and round in a recognised rut, here I am—the merest un-notorious Nobody. What a pity! I cannot but heave an involuntary sigh over my lost opportunities. If I had only had the necessary ambition, I could have been made a "Celebrity at Home" for one of the leading journals. "Fancy that!" to quote from the immortal Ibsen's "Hedda Gabler." And then—proud thought!—I should have been a Somebody. Not because I had achieved something—oh, no, that isn't required of a "Celebrity at Home." Not at all. In fact, the less you do nowadays the more likely you are to become a "celebrity" of the newspapers. So that as I have done nothing, and moreover, as I have really nothing to do, I ought, by all modern rule and plan, to be "interviewed" as—well, let me modestly suggest, as a "Coming" person, perhaps? Lots of fellows are "Coming," according to the press, who never arrive. I could be advertised as one of those, without doing much harm to anybody? Won't some one back me up? I am fully aware of the extent of my loss in literature in having failed to find a "groove"—but it's never too late to mend, and perhaps I shall discover it still and settle down in it. At present I am not anxious, because, as far as my observations on the great literary raree-show have gone, I find the chief object of the modern Pen is to earn Money, not Fame. Now, of money I have enough, and of fame—well! I am a friend of Gladstone's, and that assures fame to anybody!

X

OF THE SOCIAL ELEPHANT

U pon my word, the crowd is very dense just here! I find it more than difficult to elbow a passage through. And I know how dangerous it is to jostle literary men, even by accident—they are so touchy, that no matter how politely you apologise for the inadvertency, they never excuse it. And there is a little obstruction yonder in the person of the tame Elephant, who is a sort of grotesque pet of ours; he moves slowly on account of his bulk, and he has a big palanquin on his back in which sits the Fairy who manages him. It's quite a charming spectacle— especially the Fairy part of it—and although there is such a crush in this particular corner, it is pleasant to see how good-natured some of the people are, and how kindly they allow the Elephant to get along in spite of increasing scarcity of room, and how they all make light of his awkward size because he is such a nice, mild, innocent, sagacious creature.

What am I talking about?—who am I talking about? Nothing!— nobody! I am only making an allegory. It is not called "The Sunlight Lay Across my Bed," but "The Elephant Walked Across my Path." So he did on one occasion. I wasn't a bit inconvenienced by his proceedings; he thought I was, but I wasn't.

When they are at home the Elephant and the Fairy live together. The Elephant has a Trunk (or Intellectual Faculty) of the utmost delicacy and sensitiveness at the tip, and with this exquisitely formed member he is fond of picking up Pins. The Fairy watches him with a touch of melancholy interest in her lovely eyes; pins are certainly useful, and he does pick them up "beautifully." No one can be more bewitching than the Fairy; no one can be blander or more aware of his own value than the Elephant. Conscious of weight and ponderous movement, he nevertheless manages to preserve a suggestion of something indefinable that is "utter." He is not without malice—note the slyness of his eye when he is at his graceful trick of Pin-lifting. He will, it is true, wave his trunk to and fro with a majestic gentleness that seems harmless, but a closer inspection of him will arouse in the timorous observer a vague sense of danger. The chances are ten to one that he will accept the sugared biscuit (or compliment) offered to him by the unsuspecting beholder, and then that he will incontinently seize the unsuspecting one suddenly round the body and dash him to bits on the flat ground of some hard journalistic matter suitable for smashing a man. But he never forgets himself so far as to trumpet forth this secret capability of his; the only warning the visitor ever receives as to his possible malicious intent is the solemn twinkle of his sly green eye. Beware that eye! it means mischief.

As for the Fairy, it is not too much to say that she is one of the prettiest things alive. She does not seem to stand at all in awe of her Elephant lord. She has her own little webs to weave—silvery webs of gossamer-discussion on politics, in which, bless her heart for a charming little Radical, she works neither good nor harm. Her eyes would burn a hole through many a stern old Tory's waistcoat and make him dizzily doubtful as to what party he really belonged to for the moment. She has the prettiest hair, all loosely curling about her face, and she has a very low voice, so modulated as to seem to some folks affected in its intonation. But it isn't affected; it is a natural music, and only repulsive old spinsters with cracked vocal cords presume to cast aspersions on its dulcet sweetness. She dresses "æsthetically"—in all sorts of strange tints, and rich stuffs, made in a fashion which the masculine mind must describe as "gathered-up-anyhow"—with large and wondrous sleeves and queer mediæval adornments—it pleases her whim so to do, and it also pleases the Elephant, who is apt to get excited on the subject of Colour. We all know what a red rag is to a bull—so we should not be surprised to find an Elephant who is calmed by some colours and enraged by others. Colour, in fact, is the only rule of life accepted by the Elephant—better to have no morality, according to him, than no sense of Colour. And so the Fairy robes herself in curious and cunningly-devised hues to soothe the Elephant's nerves (Elephants have thick hides but excessively fragile nerves, as every naturalist will tell you); and pranks herself out like a flower of grace set in a queen's garden. She does not talk much, this quaint Fairy, but she looks whole histories. Her gaze is softly wistful, and often abstracted; at certain moments her spirit seems to have gone out of her on invisible wings, miles away from the Elephant and literary Castle, and it is in such moments that she looks her very prettiest. To me she is infinitely more interesting than the Elephant himself, but as it is the Elephant whom everybody goes to see, I must try to do him justice—if I can!

To begin with, I know him very well, and he knows me. I have fed him many a time and oft with the sugared compliments he likes best—and what is really a matter worth noting he has *allowed* me to feed him. This is very good of him. He is not so amiable to everybody. Few indeed are permitted the high honour of holding out a dainty morsel of flattery to that delicately-sniffing trunk which "smells a rat" too swiftly to be easily cajoled. But it has pleased the Elephant to take food from my hand, though while he ate, I noticed he never stopped winking. So that I know perfectly well who it was that lifted me up a while ago in a journal that shall be nameless, and did his utmost to smash me utterly by the force with which he threw me down again. Elephants have "nasty humours" now and then—it is their nature. But for once this particular animal found his match. He didn't hurt me though he tried; I got up from under his very feet, and—offered him another Compliment. He took it—gracefully; swallowed it "beautifully"—and does not wink quite so much now. Still, his eye is always on me—and mine on him—and we begin to understand each other.

His prettiest trick, and the one for which he is chiefly admired, is, as I said before, the delicate way in which he picks up Pins. Pins that any less sensitive creature would think worthless, he instantly perceives, selects and classes as "distinctly precious." Minute points of discussion having to do with vague subjects which (unless we could live on an Island of Dreams like the Laureate's Lotus-eaters) no one has any time to waste in considering, he (the Elephant) turns over and over and disposes of in his own peculiar fashion. He has a low estimate of man's moral responsibilities, he thinks that if the "masses" could only be brought to appreciate Colour as keenly as he himself appreciates it, the world would be both happy and wise, and would have no further need of law. He considers Nature *au naturel* a mistake. Nature must be refined by Art. *Ergo*, a grand waterfall would not appeal to him, unless properly illumined by electricity, or otherwise got up for effect. He himself is got up for effect—if he were not, according to his own showing, he would be hideous. An Elephant of the jungle is unlovely, but an Elephant in civilian attire, decently housed, with a Fairy to look after him and preside over his meals, is a very different animal. Art has refined him. Nature has nothing more to do with him.

Sometimes the Elephant ruminates. Pins cease to interest him, and with coiled-up trunk (*i.e.*, Intellectual Faculty), and heavy limbs at rest, he shuts his blinking emerald eyes to outer things, and thinks. Then,

MARIE CORELLI

rising with a mighty roar of trumpeting that blares across the old world and the new, he tears up the ground beneath his feet, and throws a Production—*i.e.*, a novel, or a play—in the face of his foes. And his foes momentarily shrink back from him, appalled at the noise he makes; but anon they rise up boldly in their puny strength to confront his ponderosity. Staves, darts, arrows and stones they get together in haste and trembling, and, shielding themselves behind different editor's desks, begin the wild affray. Lo, how the huge Trunk sways and the green eyes glare! Trample the Production to pieces, ye pigmy ruffians of reviewers, ye shall never crush what is "immortal!" Howl, ye spitfires of the Press, ye shall never make the Elephant's shadow diminish by one iota! For the fulminating truth of the elephantine Production, from a literary point of view, is this: That "as a work of art it is perfection, and perfection is what we artists aim at."

Thus the Elephant, with much pounding of feet, swinging of trunk, lashing of tail, and scattering of dust in the eyes of bewildered beholders. And truly he succeeds in attracting an infinite amount of attention, as why should he not? He is a lordly animal; large enough to be seen at a distance, and society pets him as it pets all creatures of whom it is vaguely afraid. Shy, retiring souls have no chance whatever of what is called "social success" nowadays. You must either be an Elephant or a Gnat; you must rend or sting before society will take any notice of you. And though critics curse the Elephant and wish he were well out of their way, Society fondles him; and as long as he is thus fondled, so long will he score certain victories in art and literature. It is impossible to "quash" him, he is too big. Every one is bound to look at him, and when he begins to move, albeit slowly, every one is equally bound to get out of the way.

There was once a time, however (when the Elephant was younger), in which it seemed doubtful whether he would remain an Elephant. A strange spell was upon him, a wizard-glow of the light that blinds reviewers—Genius. He stood on the confines of a sort of magic territory, wagging his delicate Trunk wistfully, and taking inquiring sniffs at the world. He was then like one of those deeply interesting animals we read about in the dear old fairy-books; he was waiting for the proper person to come and cut off his head, or throw water over him, or something, and say—"Quit thy present form and take that of a——" What? Well, let us say "Poet," for example. Yes, that would have probably been the correct formula—"Quit thy present form and take that of a Poet." And then, hey presto! he would have skipped out of his hide, all dressed in dazzling blue and silver, a very Prince of wit and wisdom. But the magician who could or might have worked this change in him didn't turn up at the right moment, and so no one would believe he was anything *but* an Elephant at last. And when he found that this was people's fixed opinion, and that nobody could be persuaded to think otherwise, he showed a few very ugly humours. He broke into the newspaper shops and went rampaging round among the pens and the ink-pots. He knocked down a few unwary authors whom he imagined stood in his way, and when they *were* down, he stamped upon them. This was not nice of him. But he ought to have known, if he had been as wise as elephants are supposed to be, that authors, unless they are very frail indeed, take a deal of killing before being killed. And he might have foreseen the possibility of those trampled people getting up and revenging themselves whenever they had the chance. His "perfect" work was the very thing they had waited for ever so long. And they did not spare the Elephant. Not they! They remembered the weight of his feet on themselves, and not being able to tread on him because he was so large and heavy and obstinate, they stuck things into him instead. The "barbëd arrow," you know, that kind of disagreeable small weapon that goes in deep and rankles. A whole shower of such irritating little darts went into the Elephant—just in the delicate fleshy places between the folds of his hide—and it was an amazing sight to see how badly he took them. Never was such a roaring and trumpeting heard before! In the unreasoning heat of rage he quite forgot how matters really stood, and that he was only getting the *quid pro quo* he actually deserved. He never gave a thought to the authors he had mangled and left for dead, and who had not been allowed to make any outcry on the subject of their wounds. He had no recollection of that Scriptural anecdote which tells how the "dry bones" came together "bone by bone," and became a "great standing army." *His* "dry bones" were the poor poets and novelists he had stamped upon; indeed, not only had he stamped upon them, but he had even filled his trunk with muddy water, and squirted it over their seemingly lifeless remains. But the "great army" was there, and not past fighting, and it marched straight at and around the Elephant. On one occasion it encamped a force against him in the *St. James's Gazette*, and alas, for the good Elephant's vanity, he imagined he had foes there simply because he holds Radical views. Ye gods! Who that is commonly sane, cares whether an elephant be Radical, Whig, or Tory? Politics are the very last subject in the world I should consult an Elephant about. The mere idea of such a thing is enough to make a certain *St. James's Gazette* reviewer I wot of, split his sides with laughter in the evil secrecy of his literary den.

As I hinted before, the Elephant while on the rampage in the newspaper-shops once chanced on my humble self, sitting back in an unobtrusive corner. One would have thought that to a lordly animal of such a size, I might have seemed too microscopic to be noticed, but not a bit of it. He "went" for me, with a good deal of unnecessary vigour—a total waste of power on his part, I considered; however, that was his look-out, not mine. He didn't know who I was then, and he doesn't quite know now, though I believe if I threw off my domino and showed him my features he would take to his old tricks again in a minute. But I don't want to irritate him, because he is really a good creature; I would much rather pet him than goad him. He can be cruel, but he can also be kind, and it is in the latter mood that everybody likes him and wants to give him sugar-candy. Moreover, as Elephant he is the living Emblem of Wisdom—a sacred being; and, if one is of an Eastern turn of mind, worthy of worship—and I never heard of any one yet who would venture to cast a doubt on his sagacity. He is wonderfully knowing; his opinion on some things is always worth having, and when he picks up Pins his movements are graceful and always worth watching. Moreover, one never gets tired of looking at the lovely Fairy who guards and guides him. We could not spare either of the twain from our midst—they form a picture "full of Colour." When we view that picture the "moral sense" of Colour enters into us—we feel twice born and twice alive. See how graceful is the *cortége*! how quaint and pretty and Oriental! Through the eye-holes of my domino I gaze admiringly upon the group—it makes a bright reflection on the "tablets of my memory." Move on, gentle Elephant! Move on! As slowly as you like, and at your own pleasure. Only don't try to "smash" me any more—it's useless. I am formed of that hard "virile" composition of literary ware "guaranteed unsmashable"—I am neither glass nor porcelain. Have another biscuit? Another *bon-bon* of sugared praise? Well, then, you are a poet in disguise—a genius, wrapped up and sealed down under a hopeless weight of circumstances. I know your buried qualities well, and had some brave person cut off your head—*i.e.* your Self-Esteem (as I previously suggested)—years ago, we might have had a Prince, nay, even a King, among us. Yet on the whole I think you are happy in your condition. The *dolce far niente* suits you very well, and the bovine repose of an almost Buddhistic meditation entirely agrees with your constitution, while as long as life lasts you may be sure you shall never lack Pins. Pass, good Elephant! I salute you profoundly, and with a still more profound reverence I kiss the hands of the Fairy!

XI

THE STORY OF A SOUTH AFRICAN DREAM

E lephants and Fairies suggest the "Arabian Nights." The "Arabian
Nights" suggest, in their turn, the East, and the East suggests—ah!
what does the East not suggest? A. P. Sinnett with his eyeglass? a vision
of "Koot-Hoomi?" pretty Mrs. Besant, once atheist, now theosophist?
or the marvellous fat (now dematerialised) of the marvellous Blavatsky?
More, far more than these things! The very idea of the East causes me
to stand still where I am, in a corner among all the literary folk, and
"dream." The mood grows upon me; I am in the humour for "dreams." I
feel metaphysical; don't listen to me; the fit will pass by and by. Nay, it
is passing, and I feel pious instead—very pious; and I shall probably get
blasphemous directly. From piety to blasphemy is but a step; from the
prayer of Moses to his professing to see the Deity's "back parts" was
but the hair's-breadth of a line in Holy Writ. And as I find everything
in a very bad state, and as I think everybody wants reforming, I am
going to tell a little story. It is a beautiful little story, and if you ask the
Athenæum about it, it will tell you that it is "like a picture by Watts";
that "it has had no forerunners in literature and probably will have no
successors." So you must pay great attention to it, and you must think it
over for a long time. It requires thinking over for a long time, because
it is a Parable. The best people, and especially those who want to "tickle
the ears" of the *Pall Mall* groundlings, are all going to talk and live and
write in Parables for the future. So listen!

> *"There was once a woman in South Africa.*
> *She saw the sunlight lie across her bed.*
> *When there is a window and no blind to it, the sunlight has*
> *a way of pouring in,*
> *And of falling in the direction which is most natural to itself.*
>
> *   *   *   *   *
>
> *The sunlight did not move,*
> *So the woman covered her eyes.*
> *And sleep came upon the woman and she dreamed.*
>
> *   *   *   *   *

Now in her dream the woman saw a hole.
It was a round hole, and it was red inside and very deep
And the woman looked down at the hole and said—
'What hole is this?'
And a loud voice answered her, saying—
'That hole is Hell!'
And the woman looked up, and, lo! there was God laughing at her.

* * * * *

And the woman looked down again at the hole, and saw how red it
was and how very deep.
And she knelt down, with both arms leaning on the brink of the hole.
And she said to God: 'I like this place.'
And God answered: 'Ay, dost thou so?'
And God laughed again.
And the woman said again: 'I like this place. It seems warm.'
And God said: 'Ay, it is *warm.'*
And the woman said: 'I think I will go in thither.'
And God said: 'Ay, go by all means!'
And the woman went.

* * * * *

The hole was very wide and red and deep.
And the woman had plenty of space to slide down.
She slid; and the hole got wider and redder and deeper, but
still she slid on.
And presently she caught a creature by the hair.
And she said to the creature: 'Who art thou?'
And the creature answered: 'I am X. Y. Z. of the Athenæum,
Bream's Buildings, Chancery Lane.
And the woman said: 'Good, I like thee. Give me thy hand,
and we will go together.'
And the creature went with the woman.

* * * * *

The hole grew deeper, and it began to be more hot than warm.
And further on the woman saw another creature saying mock prayers.
And the woman asked: 'To whom dost thou say mock prayers?'
And the creature said: 'To God up there. I want him not to laugh at me.'
Then the woman said: 'Who art thou that God should laugh?'
And the creature writhed, and answered: 'I am the religious Spirit of
the Pall Mall, *abiding in the street called Northumberland, off Strand.'*

And the woman said again: 'And doth God laugh at thee?'
And the creature answered: 'Ay, he laugheth sore.'
And the woman said: 'Nay, he shall not laugh. I will tell him
to protect thee. Come with me.'
And the creature ceased praying mock prayers, and
followed the woman.

*   *   *   *   *

And presently the woman from South Africa grew weary.
She desired to get out of the hole.
And she called aloud to God: 'I wish to leave Hell.'
And God said: 'Leave it then.'
And she left it.

Outside the sun was shining.
There was no hole anywhere to be seen.
And the woman looked up, and lo! there was God laughing at her.
Then said the woman: 'There is no hole.'
And God gaily answered, 'No.'
Then the woman asked: 'Where is Hell?'
And God, very much amused, replied: 'I haven't the least idea!'
And the woman smiled right joyously, and said: 'I have
had bad Dreams.'
And God said: 'You have!'

The sunlight lay across the bed of the woman from South Africa.
She woke, and thought of the deep red hole she had seen.
And she reflected on her strange meeting with X. Y. Z. of the
Athenæum, *and the 'Religious Spirit' of the* Pall Mall.
And she also thought what a playful and hilarious personage God was.
Then she remembered she had had late supper the previous evening.
Which accounted for 'Dreams.'

The sunlight still lies now and then across the bed of the woman
from South Africa.
It is a way the sunlight has.
And God laughs, as well He may."

Now I hope everybody sees what a "touching simplicity" there is, what a child-like familiarity with the Deity pervades the whole of this "prose poem." And yet there is a "subtlety," a candour, a strange melancholy, a curious cynicism, and a weirdness of conception and strong picturesqueness about its every line. It is unique in itself; it wants no explanation, because it says everything in the fewest words. It has a diction as innocent and unadorned as that of an infant's first spelling-book. And all the best critics I know want authors to let "brevity be the soul of wit," and to tell their stories as concisely as possible. If I were a novel-maker and wished to please the critics, I should write my "thrillers" in telegram form; twelve or twenty-four words to a chapter. Then I am sure I should get very well reviewed. Critics have no time to read any thoroughly finished and careful work—they seldom can do more than scan the first page and the last. I know this, being a Critic myself, and I think it is a thousand pities authors should take any trouble to write a middle part to their stories. An Ollendorf curtness of wording is always desirable, unless, indeed, one happens to be a George Meredith, and can manage to get cleverly involved in a long sentence which takes time to decipher, and when deciphered has literally no meaning at all. Then of course one is a genius at once; but such masterly art is rare. And so on the whole I like the "allegory" style best, because it is both brief and obscure at the same time. It has the surface appearance of simplicity, but its depth—ah! it is surprising to what a depth you can go in an allegory. You can fall down a regular well of thought and go fast asleep at the bottom, and when you wake up you wonder what it was all about, and you have to begin that allegory over again. That is what I call "reading"—hard reading—sensible reading. I like a thing you can never make head or tail of—the brain fattens on such provender. I am going to write out several dozen "Dreams" by and by—some of the queer ones I have had after a bout of champagne, for example—and I shall give them *gratis* to the *Pall Mall* with my fondest blessing. If there is "one bright particular star" in the sphere of journalism I worship more than another it is the *Pall Mall*, and I feel I can never do too much for it. And it likes "dreams" and little innocent religious allegories, because it is so good itself, and, like the boy Washington, has "never told a lie." I have always considered that the *Pall Mall* and the German Kaiser are the only two earthly institutions "God" can favour, seeing that, according to the lady from South Africa, He has taken to "laughing" at most things. It is a pleasant picture, that of God laughing—one, too, not to be found in all the Bible. There the Deity has been represented as angry, jealous, reproachful, or benignant, but it has been left to South

African literary skill to show us how He "laughed." And as the *Pall Mall* thinks it all right that He *should* laugh, why then we ought to coincide unanimously in the *Pall Mall's* opinion. Because just imagine what London would be without the *Pall Mall*! Can mind conceive a more hideous desert?—a more wildly howling desolation? We should be left friendless and all unguided without our angel of reform; our clean, white-winged, heavenly, truthful Apostle of Northumberland Street, who is always able to tell us what is good and what is bad; who can inform us all, statesmen, clerics, authors, artists, and day-labourers, exactly what we ought and what we ought not to do. In the event of another Deluge (and some of the scientists assure us we shall have it soon) I know of a way in which some few of us might be saved; that is, some few with whom "God" is delighted, such as myself and the German Kaiser. We should simply require to make friends with the *Pall Mall* staff, (several of the members are ladies, and how charming to have their society!), and build an ark out of planks from the *Pall Mall* office floors. We should then paste it all over with *Pall Mall* placards of the latest accounts of the Flood up to date of sailing, for the fishes to read, and then we should get into it; we who were the elected ones (including the Kaiser of course), and off we would go in smiling safety, secure from winds and waves, being the only "just people" left on a corrupted earth. And if in the end we found another Mount Ararat, and it were left to the governing body, *i.e.*, the *Pall Mall* staff and the German Kaiser, to begin a new world. . . O ye gods and little fishes! What a world it would be!

XII

Questioneth Concerning
the Slough of Despond

S tanding still too long is rather monotonous work. How Socrates could
have managed to remain a whole night on his feet in meditation is
one of those strange historical circumstances that have always puzzled
me. Now here have I been only a few minutes at rest; only dreaming
one little "dream" of how I, together with the Kaiser and the *Pall Mall*,
am going to set to work in the general renovation and improvement of
mankind, and yet I am as tired and bored and disposed to yawn as any
of the gaping people in the crowd who have stopped a second to listen
to me. Let me pass on, good folk!—I will e'en resume my indolent,
aimless way, for truly there are many things to be seen both wise and
wonderful, which even a strolling player would not miss. Only I will,
with everybody's good leave, avoid that black and stagnant quagmire of
literary matter that stretches its unseemly length across the social arena.
'Tis a veritable mud-trap, a dismal Slough of Despond, into which I
once fell heedlessly, all through the force of example. I saw others (some
of whom I respected) making for the Slough, and I followed. When my
friends ran to it straight and tumbled in, I did likewise, and wallowed
in the mud with those who were near and dear to me. I stayed there
heroically till I was nearly suffocated, then, unable to bear it any longer,
I made a strong effort and scrambled out, melancholy and depressed,
but—free. Free, and wise enough not to be cajoled into those black
depths again. You see I have not yet shaken off my allegorical humour,
and I am just now speaking allegorically. For the benefit of those who
are slow to perceive the "subtle" meaning of an allegory I do not mind
condescending to explain that by the Slough of Despond I mean the
great, sticky, woful, heterogeneous mass of Magazine Literature. What
is the use of it? Why is it with us? Who wants such productions as the
magazines of England, when the magazines of America can be had?
Americans know how to make their magazines interesting; Englishmen
do not. I beg some one who is well instructed in these matters to tell me
where I can find the abnormal beings who derive any real intellectual
benefit from the ponderous pages of the *Nineteenth Century*, for

example? Little Knowles sits in his editorial chair even as an angler sits by a stream, assiduously fishing for names and nothing more. He allows Gladstone to write the purest nonsense about "Dante at Oxford," simply because he *is* Gladstone. He takes poorly-written articles on public questions from lords and dukes simply because they *are* lords and dukes. Genius weighs as nothing with him—titles and passing notorieties that "draw" are everything. Then we have the *Contemporary*, the *Fortnightly*, the *New Review*, the *Quarterly*, all on the same "deadly lively" level. The *Quarterly* still boasts of its bygone villainous attack on Keats, for not so very long ago it said that it considered that in-"famous" criticism perfectly justifiable. Satisfied with itself in this regard, it praises Hall Caine! O gods of Olympus! There is also the venerable *Blackwood*, of whose mild chimney-corner prattle it were cruel to take serious observation. And there is *Temple Bar*, *The Argosy*, *London Society*, *Belgravia*, and hosts of mild imitations of these; yet taken altogether the magazines published in London do not give in their entirety half as much satisfaction or well-written information to the reader as the American *Century* magazine, or *Harper's*. This fact helps to emphasize the general "behindhand" tendency of literary things in Great Britain, as compared to those same things in America. Even the children's magazines in the "States" are interesting, and full of concise, simple, pleasantly-worded knowledge, but here, if you want pure, undiluted literary drivel, buy a child's magazine. However, it must be remembered that Americans generally, young and old, like to acquire information; perhaps they feel they do not yet know everything. The English, on the contrary, have a rooted aversion to being instructed, inasmuch as every true-born Britisher considers himself about equal to the Deity in omniscience.

Most of us, I suppose, have heard of Charles Dickens and his immortal novels, the most wholesome, humane, sympathetic, and heart-invigorating books that ever, by happy fortune, were given to the public. And I daresay we remember in "Little Dorrit" the lively young man connected with the "Circumlocution Office," who very strenuously objected to the existence of people who "wanted to know, you know." Now I am one of those people. I want to know, you know, why we should have about us all these little marshy literary mud-pools which make up the British magazine Slough of Despond. I want those curiously-minded beings who read (and buy) the magazines, and follow all the dreadful "serials" therein, to "stand forth and deliver." I want to know, you know, how they manage to do it? Whether they feel good after it? Whether they ever read anything else? And what opinions they have formed on literature by this means? Whether they accept the verse in *Temple Bar*, for example, as actual poetry? Or the short stories and articles as samples of good terse English style? Whether they find their brains developing under the fine humour of *Belgravia*? Whether their intellectual faculties are roused by a study of *The Strand Magazine* (which began well, but is now as monotonous as the rest) or *The English Illustrated*? I want to know, you know. Who laugheth at *The Idler*? Who rejoiceth in *Macmillan's*? And who on God's good earth can stand *The Novel Review*? What happy saints peruse *The Leisure Hour*?—what angels sit down to con the pages of *Cassell's Family Magazine*? Who bothereth himself with *The Bookman*? Who conceiveth it agreeable to read *Longman's* or *The Gentleman's Magazine*? There must be people who do these things; and, certainly, by a wild stretch of imagination, I can picture a fat mamma glancing casually at *Belgravia*, the while she watches her eldest girl's flirtation with a "moneyed" suitor out of the corner of her eye; I can also deem it possible that a paunchy paterfamilias might cut the pages of *Temple Bar* and hand it in as a delicate attention to his children's governess in the schoolroom. But further than this I cannot go. It may be that the magazines exist for the domestic circle only—the English domestic circle, of course. For other countries' domestic circles they would not serve. I think all those interesting females who are understood to be "good mothers," ladies with high maternal foreheads and small chins, very likely read the magazines. They do not want to study, they do not want to learn, they never require to read anything but the tamest stuff, just to pass away an hour between lunch and afternoon-tea. These are the only individuals I can connect with magazine literature. But, of course, I may be wrong. There may be intellectual persons who accept the varied utterances of the *Nineteenth Century* and *Fortnightly* as gospel. I can understand any one liking the *Review of Reviews*. That serves a purpose, and is admirably done. Apart from its adoration of the *Pall Mall Gazette*, it is really an excellently managed concern. That and the *Century* suffice me—the American *Century* I mean, not the Nineteenth Century, which will hardly enter the Twentieth. Quite recently, one Edward Delille severely slated the American press and American literature generally, with the hysterical passion of those lady-writers who, to use reviewer's parlance, "let down their back hair and scream." Rather unkind of Edward, considering that rumour asserts him to be American himself. A man should stick up for his own country or get re-nationalised. Does Delille find English magazine literature superior to that of America? If he does, he deserves his fate! Let him wallow, as I did, in the Slough of Despond, till he groweth weary, and when he crieth, "Help! release me!" let no one answer. For the Slough is the ruin of all originally-minded men; and any novelist who writes magazine serials is simply committing literary suicide. His name grows stale to the public ear, his stories lose point, his style lacks proper warmth, and his very thoughts grow crippled. In a work of true art the creator should be free as air and answerable to none, not even to that Olympian god, a magazine editor.

But because I now avoid the Slough of Despond I do not want others to avoid it. On the contrary, I love to see a certain class of folk stuck in the mud. I feel they could not be in a better plight, and I enjoy the spectacle. Moreover, "by their magazines ye shall know them." Their conversation, their ideas, their opinions, all are taken out of the magazines. This is beautiful and edifying. The lady who talks *Temple Bar* has naturally a calmer view of life than the gentleman who talks *Nineteenth Century*. The sweet thing who murmurs *Chambers's Journal* is not so worldly-wise as her friend who utters *New Review*. The man at the club who converses *Quarterly* may or may not agree with him who pronounceth *Contemporary*. And so on. It is like the Baths of Leuk, where every mud-bather has, if he likes, his own private floating-table, with writing materials and cup of coffee. But the mud is everywhere all the same, and every man is stuck in it like a sort of civilised tadpole. And what is always a mystery to me is how so many magazines manage to "pay." For of course they must pay, or else they would not be kept going. However, there are various such social mysteries, which not even the most astute person can fathom. And I am not astute. I simply "notice" things. As for attempting to take any sort of correct measure of the fancies and "fads" of the British Public, that is impossible. Such humours are more "occult" than theosophy itself. Frenchmen cannot understand "Madame Grundée." Neither can I. She is always an incomprehensible old lady at the best of times, but when she takes to reading all the magazines and liking the literature therein contained, she becomes a spectacled Sphinx, the riddle of whose social existence is not worth the solving. And in its bovine tolerance of such an excess of stupid ephemeral literary matter Great Britain proves for the millionth time how *un*-literary and inartistic it is as a nation. But I am not going to be angry about it. I always laugh at these things. They do not affect me personally, as I am out of them. And I must never forget that I have reason to be grateful to at least one magazine out of the mass—*The Fortnightly*. It was lent to me by a friend as a cure for insomnia. It succeeded perfectly. Three pages of a long political article sufficed; a gentle drowsiness stole over me, a misty vagueness possessed my brain, and I, who had been restless for many nights, now under the somnolent spell of excellent Frank Harris, slept the sleep of the just. Others have derived the same benefit by the same means, so I am told, wherefore Harris is a benefactor to his kind. His magazine is the one little oasis in the Slough where tired folks may find rest, if not refreshment, and people who want a peaceful nap should go there straight. As for me, I am out of the Slough altogether—I merely stand near the brink and look on. And my observations are addressed to nobody. I soliloquise for my own pleasure, like Hamlet, and, with that psychological Dane, may assure everybody who is concerned about me that "I am only mad nor-nor-east; when the wind blows southerly I know a hawk from a heron-shaw."

XIII

Describeth the Pious Publisher

The pious publisher is a man who always says "God bless you!" to the author he is cheating. "God bless you!" is easily said, sounds well, and costs nothing, all of which is important. The more "profit" the pious publisher can make out of the individual he blesses, the more fervent is his benediction. Now, it is not pleasant to have to mistrust a blessing, and yet, out of the vague interest I have always taken in all human imps born of the ink-pot, I would advise them not to bow with too much childlike humility and confidence to the blessing of the pious publisher. If it is a particularly earnest and friendly benediction,— well! it might be advisable to see how "royalties" are getting on. The pious publisher does not bless you for nothing, depend upon it. You are not his relative; he has no cause to love you or ask the Almighty to look after you, unless he is making a "good thing" out of you, in which case he is grateful, after a peculiar manner of his own. Perhaps he feels he can order a few dozen extra old brands of port; perhaps, too, he will find it possible to have a certain improvement carried out in his dwelling which he has long meditated, all through you—you, a successful author whose books have had an extra large sale unknown to yourself. And, naturally, he looks at you with a moist and kindly eye; his heart swells paternally, and the blessing rises to his lips almost involuntarily. He surveys with gentle complacency the modest arrangements of your house—the tact by which worn-out furniture is concealed by "art" antimacassars, the efforts to "make both ends meet" which are proudly visible in every room, and he grows blander and blander. He admires the "art" coverings—he admires the furniture—he admires everything. He does not mind lunching with you—oh, not at all. And while at luncheon he advises you, patronisingly, sagely, as to how you should write your next book. You have your own ideas—yes, yes, that is right, that is very good! it is proper for you to have your own ideas, but it is also advisable for you to bring those ideas into keeping with the ordinary public taste. Ordinary, mark you! not extraordinary. There are certain subjects you should try to avoid, as being unpleasing to the mind of the respectable middle classes. For example, new notions with regard to religion are dangerous! yes, yes, dangerous and doubtful too—doubtful as regards a "sale." Then, bigamy is not a pleasant subject. It would cause eruptions to break out on the cheek of the Young Person, and it would not secure any chance as a "gift-book." Then, a murder is a painful thing!—exceedingly painful—you must leave out murder. And, for Heaven's sake, do not enter into any question of suicide—it is a morbid taste, and a book dealing with it in any powerful or striking manner would be quite tabooed from the middle-class family circle, especially in the provinces. A forgery might be introduced, if the forger turned out to be a manly hero in the end and properly repentant—and a little (the pious publisher would say "a leetle") illicit love would not be objectionable—in fact, it might be made highly saleable if a curate and a housemaid were the guilty parties, and there were a child born who turned out to be the heir to five millions, and the erring curate set things right in the usual thirty-one-and-sixpenny way. But nothing should be drawn too strong; you understand? no luscious colouring of any sort—keep the imagination well in check—tint the canvas grey— and make the book one that will be bought by stout, moral-minded parents, for slim, no-minded young women, and it is sure of a sale— sure! And thus the pious publisher pleasantly adviseth, the while the heart of the listening author sinks lower and lower, and his soul sickens, gasping for the strong, broad eagle freedom of flight, which while he works for a pious publisher never will be his.

It is a curious fact, but the pious publisher apparently possesses a very naïve, innocent, and undefiled nature. He does not know the world at all, or if he does, he has no idea of its wickedness. When he is told of some dreadful social scandal he does not believe it—dear, dear no! he cannot believe it. He is a round, paunchy man, is the pious publisher, bald-headed, clean-shaven, with an eminently respectable expression of countenance, and an ostentatious assertion of honesty in the very set of his clothes. He has a soft voice and a conciliating smile, and he gets on best with women authors. He tells them first how well they are looking—his next step is to call them "my dear." They are frequently much touched by this, and in the yielding softness of their hearts, forget to nail him down to "terms." Even the fiercest, ugliest "blue-stocking" that ever lived is conscious of a nervous quiver through the iron fibres of her soul, when the fat, unctuous, kindly, pious publisher, unawed by her stern features, says "My dear." There is a delicate something in his tone which pleasantly persuades her that, after all, it is possible she may be good-looking. Unconsciously she relaxes in severity, and he drives his bargain home with such sweet firmness as to entirely succeed in having his own way—a way which, whether it lead to advantage or loss, she, poor "blue," is generally too weak to dispute. "My dear" is a phrase that will not work on the minds of men authors of course, so the pious publisher, when he has to do with the "virile" sex, substitutes "My boy!" and accompanies this epithet with a hearty, encouraging clap on the shoulder. When the author in question is too old and frail (as well as too reduced to misery by the machinations of pious publishers) to be impressed by this jovial "My boy!" the pious publisher is not at a loss. No! He then says "My dear fellow," in gentle, serious, sympathetic accents. This frequently produces a good effect. It is indeed remarkable what an impression these meaningless, apparently kindly, short phrases have on the weary minds of authors when uttered by the pious publisher. It is ridiculous in a way, but pitiful too. No consciousness of intellectual supremacy will ever eradicate from the human heart the craving for human sympathy, and the biggest author that ever wielded potent pen has no proof-armour against the simple magic of a kindly word. And tired out with long thinking and labour, it may be that sometimes the pious publisher's "dear fellow" hits a sensitive little place in the author's complex mechanism, somewhere about where the tears are (if any author is permitted to have tears), and he becomes dimly soothed by the simple phrase, so soothed as to actually fancy he has found—a friend! And in the little "arrangement" made for his work the pious publisher scores again—heavily, as usual.

Needless to say the pious publisher is an exceedingly shrewd business man. His piety distinctly "pays." His "God bless you!" has saved him many an extra twenty or fifty pounds; his "my dear" and "dear fellow" have helped to make suspicious novelists accept without a murmur his statements of their royalties. He knows all this perfectly well. He reads all the poor, pitiful, yet beautiful human weakness of men and women thoroughly, and makes his capital out of it while he can. God, we are told, compassionates human weakness; the pious publisher lives by it. He uses the sad little vanities of the would-be "genius" as so many channels of speculation. He has an agreeable way of reminding the very small writer of the gloriously self-denying manner in which the very great writers managed to exist—those writers of old historic time who served Art for Art's sake, and were content to live upon a crust of bread for the sake of future glory. That noble Crust!

The pious publisher wishes all authors would live upon it. "My dear boy," he says, "it is the modern thirst of gold that kills Art. Now you are a true 'artist.'" (Here probably the small writer thus addressed cannot restrain a nervous wriggle of satisfaction.) "Yes, yes! a true artist! I can see that at a glance. To you money weighs as nothing compared with high ambition and attainment." (The small writer is perhaps not quite sure about this, still he is unable to look stern, so he smiles feebly.) "To grind out literature for the mere sake of accumulating cash would be distasteful to a man of your lofty spirit. You were made for better things. The notorieties of the day who allow themselves to be paragraphed and 'boomed' and all the rest of it, and command for the moment large sales, are really mere ephemera. Now, my dear boy, let me advise you not to hamper your evident genius by over-anxiety about money. Do your work, the great work that is in you to do; and if the rewards come slowly, never mind! in your old age you will look back to these days of effort as the sweetest of your life! Yes!" and the pious publisher's eyes moisten at his own eloquence, "in the sunset of your career, when you have made an assured name, and, let us hope, an assured fortune also, you will remember this time of grand struggle and endeavour! God bless you!"

The benediction is here uttered abruptly, as if the pious publisher couldn't help it. It bursts from his manly bosom like a bomb-shell. His pent-up emotion finds vent in it; his swelling liberality of disposition is relieved by it. Meanwhile, the small author sits silent, curiously disconcerted, and uncomfortably conscious that his face wears a somewhat foolish expression. He doesn't want to look foolish, but he knows he does. He is aware that the pious publisher has flattered him, but somehow he does not like to admit that the flattery is more than kindly and judicious praise. But, all the same, he ponders in a dismal sort of way on those phrases "in your old age" and "the sunset of your career." What! Is he, then, not to experience any of the joys or luxuries of life till he is such a doddering old idiot as to be only fit to jabber "reminiscences"? Is he to have no rest or physical comfort in existence till his strength fails and his mental faculties decay? Is his fortune only to be "assured" at a time when his chief needs are a bed, an armchair, and a basin of gruel or "infant's food"? The pious publisher implies as much. It is strange, and perhaps wickedly ungrateful of the poor small author, but he does not care about the "sunset" prospect in the least. He would rather be happy and well fed while it is full day. And for the life of him he cannot help thinking how very excellently the pious publisher himself is housed. Pictures, books, statuary, horses—even a yacht—all these things have come to the pious publisher long before "sunset." And yet what can he, the poor small author, do? Nothing. He must consider himself lucky if he gets his work accepted on any terms. He can't afford to be his own publisher (not because of the expenses incurred in actually printing and binding, for these are slight), but because he would be considered an intruder and would have all the "publishers' rings" against him; and not only the publishers' rings, but the Circulating Library Ring and the Bookstall Ring; for England is a "free" country, and as a first consequence of its glorious liberty, every one that does honest work and seeks honest pay for the same, is the veriest slave that ever wore chains and manacles.

There are many publishers, of course, who are not pious, and these are generally among the most honest of their class. They do not pretend to be anything but tradesmen, with an eye to business, and no taste whatever for literature *as* literature. They would as soon be cheesemongers if the book-trade failed. They affect nothing; they are brusque, commonplace men, and they often play a losing game by their lack of proper urbanity. The pious publisher never loses a farthing. He is always lining and re-lining his nest. He issues a larger number of works by women than by men, for the reason that women are more unbusinesslike than their lords, and more easily persuaded to accept starvation prices. It may be said, and rightly, that women's work is not frequently worth much, but there are, at the present time, two or three women in literature whose success is indubitable and whose names alone are of market value. These are they whom the pious publisher loves to secure. The more gifted they are, the more unpractical; the more engrossed in imaginative conception, the more unconscious of treachery. They perhaps feel the pious publisher is even as a father to them. He is invariably kind and courteous, and is always able to "explain" troublesome things with the involved eloquence of a Gladstone. Indeed, it can never be said that either to man or woman at any time has the pious publisher been dictatorial or unfriendly. He is too bland, too conscious of rectitude, too innocent of the world's evil to be capable of anything but the truest Christian behaviour. If a long-suffering author were to quarrel with him, he would only mildly "regret the rupture of friendly terms," while quietly letting all his particular "ring" know of the "rupture," and warning them against having to do with the quarrelsome author in question; for the pious publisher has no scruple in "boycotting" an author who deserts him for a rival house. He can do so if he likes, and he frequently does like. Did you not know this before, O ye unworldly, simple-minded Pensters? Then know it now on the faith of a wandering truth-teller, and beware of getting twisted in the pious publisher's silken coils. Stand firm without yielding under his friendly shoulder-blow; turn his terms of endearment into terms of ready cash, and if you succeed in making a good bargain you may be sure he will *not* say, "God bless you!" He will probably sigh and tell you he is a poor man. This is a promising sign for you, and you can bless *him* if you like. But, unless you are willing to be "done," never under any circumstances allow him to bless *you*. Most casual benedictions are of doubtful value, but the blessing of the pious publisher is, financially speaking, an author's damnation. Beware it therefore; go on unblessed, and prosper!

XIV

OF CERTAIN GREAT POETS

S top, stop, my dear Lord Tennyson! Whither away so fast? Why turn your back churlishly upon me?—why spoil dignity by hastening your steps?—why hide that venerable and honoured head in a hermit's cowl of distrust for all human kind? I am not the "ubiquitous interviewer"; I do not want a lock of your hair or your autograph, for the autograph I have in your own letters, and certainly you cannot spare any hair just now. Fear me not, then, O great but crusty Poet; my silver domino conceals the features of a friend; I will do no more than render you distant but most absolute homage. I would not pry into your garden solitudes at Haslemere—no, not for the '*World*.' I would not force my way into your little kingdom at Freshwater for anything an enterprising editor might offer me; for I love you as all England loves you, and the utmost I can wish is that you would be friends with both me and England. What have we done to you, my dear Lord—peer of the realm and Peer of Poets—that you should disdain us, every one, and take so much precaution to avoid our company? Have we not, as it were, fallen at your feet in worship?—marked you out in our hearts and histories as the greatest poet of the Victorian Era, and taken pride in the splendour of your fame? Despise us not, noble Singer of sweet idylls, for remember we have never despised *you*. In our troubles and losses we have dropped soft tears over "In Memoriam"; in our loves and hopes we have wandered among the woods and fields, singing in thought the songs of "Maud" and "The Princess"; in our dreamy moods we have pored over "The Lotus-Eaters," "The Palace of Art," "Tithonus," or "Ænone"; in our passionate moments we have felt all the scorn and burning sorrow pent up in "Locksley Hall." You are the divine melodist who has set our deep-hidden English romance and sentiment to most tenderly expressed music; we are grateful, and we have shown our gratitude. We have given you such fond hearing as few poets ever win; we have lodged you in fair domains, and guarded you as a precious jewel of the realm. What can we do more to satisfy you? Is there any grander guerdon for a poet's labour than the whole English-speaking people's honour? And that you have; and yet you manifest a soured discontent that sadly misfits your calling. What is it all about? You do not want to be looked at—"stared at" is your own way of expressing it—you do not wish to be spoken to—you desire to ignore those who most reverence you, and you treat with ill-mannered, "touch-me-not" disdain the very people whose faithful admiration gives you all the good things of this life which you enjoy. Oh, petulant Poet-peer! Do no memories of the great dead bards (greater in genius than yourself, but less fortunate in their reward) sometimes flit like ghosts across the horizon of your dreams? Of Chatterton, self-slain through biting poverty; of Keats, dying before he reached his prime, while on the very verge of the promised land of Fame; of Byron, self-exiled, his splendid muse embittered by private woes; of Shelley, piteously drowned before he had time to measure his own vast intellectual forces?—while you, my good Lord, fostered by a nation's love and recognition, have experienced no such cutting cruelties at the hand of destiny. Perhaps, indeed, you have been too fortunate, and continuous prosperity has made you careless and over-easily satisfied with the lightest trifle of verse that suggests itself to your fancy. But if you are careless, you need not be crusty. The British Public has been likened unto an Ass by many, but to my thinking it is more like a dog—an honest, good-natured dog who never bites except under the severest and most repeated provocation. As a dog it has fawned at your footstool, looked up in your eyes affectionately and wagged its tail persistently—have you no other response to such fidelity save a kick or a blow? Oh, fie on such ill-humour—such uncalled-for cantankerousness! Why should you seek to be "protected" from those who would fain do you honour? We should all like to see you sometimes, in society, at theatre or opera, at flower-show and harmless festival; we should like to say to one another on beholding you, "There is our Laureate—our grand old Tennyson, one of the glories of England!" We should not harm you by our affection. We have no design upon your life, save to pray that it may be guarded and prolonged. Believe me, it would be far more natural, and, let me add, more Christian (for I knew by your noble lines "Across the Bar" that you have not smirched your white flag of song with the ugly blot of atheism) if you could persuade the world to understand that a journey or a sea-voyage in the company of England's Laureate, were it possible to devise such an out-of-the-way form of pleasure, would be one of the most cheery, prosperous, and ideal trips ever made; that the heart of the great poet-thinker was so expansive and warm, that even the tiny, toddling children adored him; that his sympathy was so vast that the poorest and most unhappy scribbler alive was sure to have a genial word from the "singing lips that speak no guile"—in brief, that every soul on board the good ship sailing sunwards, must needs be better, happier, wiser, and more full of the milk of human kindness for those few days passed in the near presence of the golden-voiced Minstrel of the legended Arthur's court. Why, good my Lord Alfred, should you, of all people in the world, preach and not practise? You, whose majestic figure seems already receding from us through the opening portals of the Unknown—why should you not stretch out hands of benediction on us ere you go? You are leaving us for other lands, dear Poet, and we all stand gazing after you sorrowfully, waving "farewell!" while the fond and foolish women we love, waft you kisses amid their tears; praise and thanks and blessings to the last from us, my Lord—and will you give us nothing better at parting than a frown? Of a truth there are countless worlds in the universe beside this one; only we cannot follow you where you are going, and so we know not whether you may find a kingdom in the stars better than Shakespeare's England. But whatsoever is deemed the highest reward among high Immortals, that reward we desire may be yours; for all the happiness which pure thoughts, sweet music, and tender song can give, you have given to the little country you are soon to see the last of. The end is not yet indeed, but it is nigh.

It is not the people, my Lord, the people on whom you have bestowed the life-long fruits of your genius, who are to blame for the grossly ill-judged and indelicate speculations that have lately been rife as to who shall occupy your throne and wear your crown, when you shall have resigned both for larger labours. It is the Press, with which the people have really nothing to do. And as to the Laureateship, I, like every one else, have my ideas, not of putting in a claim for the post, (though I could, at a push, write blank verse, quite as prettily and inanely as Lewis Morris), but of making it of wider application. After yourself I consider that no one should be permitted to hold it as you have done for an entire lifetime. It should be given to the deserving bard for five or seven years, no longer; and at each expiration of the appointed period there should be a brisk competition for the right of succession. Such an arrangement would give a great impetus to literature generally, and the recurring competitions would waken up society to a sense of artistic feeling and excitement. Moreover, to keep pace with the demands of the time, when the people are supposed to be worthy of having a voice in everything, the election of England's Laureate should be voted for by England's Public, and not left to the decision of a Clique. Cliquism would put an end to all possibility of fair play or justice, as it always does. To keep this public judgment up to a certain intellectual standard, every householder paying rent and taxes amounting together to not less than £200 per annum, should have a vote; and, because women are frequently the best readers and judges of poetry, one woman in every such household should also be entitled to a vote. The result of the plan would be that by degrees society would become interested in Poetry, which by tradition and heritage is distinctly the first of the Fine Arts—and would take pains to understand it, by which piece of additional education nothing would be lost to civilisation, but rather much might be gained in gentleness, quick perception, and fine feeling. It would be a safer and more respectable line of study at any rate than turf speculations. But, like all good ideas, it will, I suppose, have no chance of acceptance, in which case, rather than see inferior men, like Morris or Edwin Arnold, in the position which you, my Lord, have so greatly dignified, I would say with others whom I know, "Abolish the post, and let Tennyson be our last Laureate." For there is no one fitted to occupy it after you, unless it be some singer unknown to the Log-rolling community. Therefore, it would be best for England, in losing you, to also lose the very name of Laureate, save as a noble and unsullied memory.

You see how truly my devotion turns towards you, my dear Lord, though you will have none of it, nor of any such "outside vulgar" sympathy. A recent letter of yours to me contains the following sentence: "*I sometimes wish I had never written a line.*" Alas, good Nestor among modern bards, has Fame brought no happier end than this? No more than spleen and peevishness? Suppose, for sake of argument, this curious wish of yours had been granted, and you had never "*written a line.*" Well? What of the glory of renown?—what of the peerage which descends, a poet's mantle, on your heirs? what of the creature comforts of Haslemere and Freshwater?—what of the good honest cash that is paid for every airy rhyme that is blown from your imagination as lightly as the winged pine-seed from its cone? If you had "*never written a line,*" would you have gained anything? Nay, surely you would have lost much. Therefore, why carp and cavil in the radiant face of Fortune, the smiling goddess who has never deserted you since the publication of your first volume? Cheerly, cheerly, good heart! Lift up your head and look frank kindness on the world! It is not a bad world after all, and whatever its faults, it loves you. Let it see you at your best and friendliest before you say "Good-bye!"

When I was very youthful and imaginative, I used to believe implicitly in that old fairy legend (known to Shakespeare as well as myself) which declares that toads "ugly and venomous" have precious jewels in their heads. And I had a special partiality for toads in consequence. I used to assist them respectfully with a stick when they came panting out under the leaves in hot weather in search of water, and guide them gently towards the object of their desires. When a toad stared at me fixedly with his peculiarly bright eyes, I felt vaguely flattered. I had an idea that perhaps he might be intellectually capable of making a will and leaving me his brain-jewel. Needless to say I was disappointed; no toad ever fulfilled the hopes I had of him. But since those green and happy days I have gained an insight into the hidden meaning of the fable—which is, of course, that unfascinating and personally disappointing individuals may possess the greatest intellectual powers. Now there is one man who is distinctly inimical to me, personally speaking, and yet I am fain to do his "brain-jewel" justice. I allude to Algernon Charles Swinburne, whom, to meet on his way to and from "The Pines," Putney, serves as a revelation. The first impression one gets is of a small man with large feet, walking as if for a wager, arms swinging hither and thither, and fingers briskly playing imaginary tunes in the air as he goes. Then, as the eccentric shape comes nearer, one is aware of a stubbly beard, and peeping eyes expressive of mingled distrust and aversion; a hideous hat is clapped down over the broad brow, which hat when lifted displays a bald expanse of skull bearing no sort of resemblance whatever to the counterfeit presentments of Apollo, and yet, incongruous though it seem, this little, nervous, impatient, querulous being is no other than the author of the "Triumph of Time," one of the finest poems in the English language; and these twiddling restless fingers penned the majestic, burning, beautiful "Tristram of Lyonesse," a book which, like an imperial jewel-casket, is literally piled with gems. To look at the man and to think of his poems at the same time is enough to make one gasp for breath. It appears quite impossible to realise that this solitary biped trotting full speed to Wimbledon should have written such lines as these:—

> "I shall never be friends again with roses,
> I shall loathe sweet tunes, where a note grown strong
> Relents and recoils, and climbs and closes,
> As a wave of the sea turned back by song."

One can, however, easily believe that he wrote of himself in the following passage:—

> "But who now on earth need care how I live?
> *Have the high gods anything left to give*
> *Save dust and laurels and gold and sand?*
> *Which gifts are goodly; but I will none.*"

Swinburne, like Tennyson, manifests a great abhorrence for the society of his fellow-creatures, but his shrinking churlishness is more accountable to the world than that of the elder bard. Tennyson's muse is pure, refined, and ever persuasive to good; while at times Swinburne seems possessed of a very devil of lewdness and atheism; and lewdness and atheism are not yet openly accepted as desirable parts of a liberal education. Of his former rank and rampant republicanism nothing need be said; the politics of a poet are always the most absurd and shifty part of him. And though lewdness of the pen is beginning to be more tolerated than once it was, thanks to the importation of such foreign trash as the "Kreutzer Sonata" and other publications of a like free-and-easy pruriency, the love of moral filth is not yet universal. We are dabbling in mire, but we do not willingly wallow in it—at least, not at present. The honest British guffaw of laughter that greets crazy old Ibsen's contemptible delineations of women, has a jovial wholesome music in it which the caterwauling of cliques cannot silence. And there is a strong under-current of feeling in the peoples of nearly all countries, that whatever prose-writers may choose to do by way of degrading themselves and their profession, poets should draw the line somewhere. Poor paralytic old Mrs. Grundy still pretends, in the most ridiculously senile way, to be quite shocked at the idea of reading "Don Juan," when, as a matter of fact, she has put on strong spectacles over her blear eyes in order to gloat upon far worse literary provender. There is not a line that Byron ever wrote approaching to the revolting indecency of Swinburne's "Faustine"—a most disgusting set of bad verses, let me tell Algernon, with my frankest compliments. The only excuse that can be offered for such a sickening affront to the very name of poetry, is that the writer must have been suffering at the time he wrote it from a sort of moral disease.

From moral disease no moral health can come—and in spite of Swinburne's unquestioned and unquestionable genius, I believe his fame will perish as utterly and hopelessly as a brilliant torch plunged suddenly in the sea. There is no stamina in him—nothing to hold or to keep in all this meteor-like shower of words upon words, thoughts upon thoughts, similes upon similes; there lacks steadiness in the music; none of the vast eternal underthrobbings of nature give truth or grandeur to the strain. It is the harsh raving and shrill chanting of a man in fever and delirium; not the rich pulsing rhythm of a singer in noble accord with life, love, and labour.

One of the most unpleasant characteristics of Swinburne's muse is the idea conveyed therein of the sex feminine. Women are no better (and rather worse) than wild animals according to this poet's standard; or if not animals, passive creatures, to be "bitten" and "sucked" and "pressed" and "crushed" as though they were a peculiar species of grape for man's special eating. Their hair is "woven and unwoven" recklessly till one feels it must surely be plucked out by the roots; their "flanks" are supposed to "shine," their "eyelids" are "as sweet savour issuing;" and the following vaguely comic lines occur in "Anactoria":—

> *"Ah, ah, thy beauty!* like a beast it bites,
> *Stings like an adder, like an arrow smites.*
> *Ah, sweet, and sweet again, and* seven times sweet
> The paces and the pauses of thy feet!"

More preposterously insane nonsense than this it would be difficult to find on any printed page extant.

It will be chiefly on account of his utterly false conception of life and the higher emotions of the human heart, that Swinburne will not leave the great name he might have left had he recognised the full dignity of his calling. He had the power, but not the will. I say he "had" advisedly, because he has it no longer. His last productions are positively puerile as compared with his first, and each new thing he writes shows the falling-off in his skill more and more perceptibly. His similes are heavy and confused; his strained efforts at impossible paradox almost ludicrous. This is the kind of thing he revels in:—

> *The formless form of a mouthless mouth,*
> *And the biteless bite of a tooth that has gone.*

We are, perforce, thrown back on the "Poems and Ballads" and "Tristram of Lyonesse," compelled to realise that in these two books we have got all of Swinburne that we shall ever get worth reading—all the concentrated fire of that genius which is dying out day by day into dull ashes. Theodore Watts, practical, friendly Watts, something of a poet himself in a grave and lumbersome way, can do nothing to revive that once brilliant if lurid glow that animated Algernon's formerly reckless spirit. It is all over—the lamp is quenched, and the harp is broken. It would have been almost better for Swinburne's fame had he died in his youth, consumed, like the fabled Phœnix, by the fierce glare of the poetic hell-flames he had kindled about himself, rather than have lived till now to drivel into a silly dotage of roundels concerning babies' toes and noses and fingers, which are assuredly the most uninteresting subject-matter to the lover of true poesy. His attempts, too, in the "Border-Ballad" style are the weakest and most unsatisfactory imitations of the rough but vigorous original models. And while on the subject of imitation, it is rather interesting to the careful student of poetic "style" to read the admirable translations made from the earlier Italian poets by Dante Gabriel Rossetti, and compare them with some of Swinburne's earlier pieces. It will be remembered that Swinburne was at one time of his life much in the company of Rossetti, and he would most probably have heard many of these translations read before they were published; anyway, the similitude of measure and rhythm between Rossetti's "renderings" and Swinburne's "originals" is somewhat striking.

Personally, I am inclined to think that the worthy Algernon Charles caught his particular trick of rhyming and rounding his verse in the fashion now known as "Swinburnian" entirely from the Italian school of Guido Cavalcanti, Rinaldo D'Aquino, and others of their time, as well as from a few old French models of the François Villon type. His actual masterpiece, a work which contains no such borrowed juggleries of rhyme, is "Tristram of Lyonesse." This great poem is not half so well known as it ought to be—most people appear never to have heard of it, much less to have read it. In perusing its pages, one scarcely thinks of the author save as the merest human phonograph through which Inspiration speaks—in fact, it is rather curious to realise how little we really do take the personal Swinburne into our consideration while reading his works, or for that matter the personal anybody who has ever done anything. Personalities are very seldom really interesting. It is only when we have a wild, wicked Byron that we are fascinated by "personality"; a man who turns upon us, saying that he is—

"only not to desperation driven,
Because not altogether of such clay
As rots into the souls of those whom I survey."

Well, well! And what of Browning? Why, Browning is dead. Moreover, he is buried in damp, dirty, evil-smelling Westminster Abbey. What more would you have for him? Fame? Let be, let be; he had Notoriety. That must suffice, and that being done, why, all is done, and there is no more to be said. Notoriety is not Fame. Fame is not Notoriety. No man can have both, though he may cheat himself into taking the lesser for the greater, and die happy in the pleasing delusion. Even so Browning died; even so was he honourably interred. May he rest in peace. Amen.

XV

OF MORE POETS

Are there no other poets in the crowd save Tennyson and Swinburne? God bless my soul, you don't suppose I am going to offend a whole mob of verse-writers—no other poets? Of course there are others! no end of others. Poets over-run our land even as the locusts over-ran Egypt, and they are all "as good, and a darned sight better," as the Yankees say, than either the Laureate or Algernon Charles, in their own opinion. Mark that last clause, please; it is important. The number of "poets" so styled by themselves is legion; only I, who am a rudely-opiniated and fastidious masquer, decline to recognise their clamorous claims to the deathless laurel. But this does not matter. Who cares what I either decline or accept? My opinions are "nothing to nobody." I only express them for my own satisfaction and amusement; I have no other good to gain thereby. As for the chance of offending the "poets" alluded to, I certainly care not a jot. I have no desire to please them in any way, as I consider most of them an offence and an obstruction in literature. Some people run away with the notion that Edwin Arnold (I give him the full glory of his "Sir" and C.S.I. elsewhere) is a poet. Certainly his books sell. The "Light of Asia," with all its best bits taken out of the original "Mahabhârata," is a perfect triumph of verse-making. All the religious ladies read it because it is so very unexciting and heavenly and harmless, and because, like all pious poetry, it preaches virtue that no one ever dreams of practising. It is a capital book for school prizes, too; it will not hurt any boy or girl to read it, and it may providentially check them in time from trying to write verse themselves. As for the "Light of the World," it will probably meet with the same success among the same class of readers, though it is much inferior to the "Light of Asia," owing to having no "Mahabhârata" in it. But Lewis Morris is quite as great a favourite with the "goodys" of society as Sir Edwin. The "goodys" don't know, and don't want to know, anything about Dante's "Inferno," and are therefore quite satisfied to accept "The Epic of Hades" as *bonâ fide* "original" matter,—and there are some "sweetly pretty" lines in "A Vision of Saints." Both productions are well adapted for gift-books, and will suit the taste of the demure provincial "misses" who wish to be discovered reading poetry under a shady tree what time the bachelor curate of the parish passeth by. All the same, I, who am a Nobody, decline to consider either Morris or Arnold poets. They are excellent verse-compilers though, and suit the tastes of those who do not care about either originality or inspiration.

I am nothing if not eccentric, and so I am disposed to place one Alfred C. Calmour among the poets. He has published no poems—he has only produced "poetical" plays, failures all, save "The Amber Heart," and he has been generally "sent to the right about" by persons with infinitely less brain than himself. It is curious to observe what spite and meanness waken in the manly breasts of certain of his fellows at the mere mention of his name. I spoke in praise of "The Amber Heart" on one occasion to a critical brother, and he at once said—"All filched out of Wills's waste-paper basket; he was Wills's secretary." "What of 'Cyrene'?" I asked. "Oh, I don't know anything about 'Cyrene'; but if there's anything good in it, depend upon it, it is stolen from Wills." I relapsed into silence, for I never thought and never shall think anything of Wills, whereas I do think something of Calmour. He is writing a drama, I hear, on "Dante and Beatrice," and I confess to anticipating it with intense interest. I want him to do as my dear friend Oscar Wilde has done—pulverise his enemies by a big success. And why? Because I hate to see a hard-working man "sat upon." And Calmour does work hard, lives hard too, and never complains or "girds" at fate, wherefore I venture to prophecy fame for him one of these days. I have been assured he is conceited. I have never found him so. Suppose he were, is conceit a singular fault in authors? Are we to believe that they are more boastfully disposed than actors, for instance?

"What do you think of Calmour?" I asked E. S. Willard on one occasion, when, in all the grave consciousness of "looking" *Judah* to the life, he stood beside me sipping convivial tea in Wilson Barrett's drawing-room.

"Think of Calmour?" he replied, with an inimitable air of self-sufficiency. "I never think of Calmour!"

Magnificent wind-bag assertiveness! but hopelessly unreasonable. Calmour is more worth thinking about than Willard, only Willard doesn't see it. The creator of a part merits greater consideration than the mime who performs it. I confess to being a lover of fair play, and when a lot of people try to "hustle" a man, I am disposed to fight for him. Anyway, Calmour has a clean and delicate pen, and does not pander to vulgar vice like that wretched old Scandinavian humbug, Ibsen. Why we should abuse Calmour and praise Ibsen passes my comprehension. Except that "foreign" scribblers are all "geniuses" with us at once—they must be, you know, simply because they *are* foreign; they have a "subtlety," a "flavour," an "ardour," a "naturalism," and—a Nastiness which is not the legitimate inheritance of the English School. Had any one of our own men dared to offer us a "Hedda Gabler," or a "Rosmersholm," or Maeterlinck's piece of bathos, "L'intruse," he would have been shrieked and howled down with derisive laughter.

I often wonder what on earth the faddists of the poor old doddering, doting *Athenæum* mean by poking and prodding about for sparks of genius in their new "heavy man," William Watson? It is very funny to call him a poet—very funny, indeed. He is a sort of fifth-rate Wordsworth—and while we can just stand the sonnets and shorter poems of Wordsworth at first-hand, a diluted example of his pattern in these days is too much for our patience. I know a good many people— in fact, I meet in social intercourse nearly everybody worth knowing— but as yet I have come upon nobody who reads Watson's poems, or who appear to know anything about Watson. Curious, isn't it? The *Athenæum* seems to carry no conviction whatever to the Ass-public.

Messrs. Trübner sent to me some time ago a book of poems, which first surprised and then fascinated me into the belief that I had discovered an English Petrarch. I think I have, too. If absolute music, perfect rhythm, and exquisite wording of love-thoughts are Petrarchian, then my man is a Petrarch. His book is called "A Lover's Litanies," and the "litanies" are the poems. There are ten of them, and each one has a title borrowed from the old church missal—rather a quaint idea. It would be difficult to match the one called "Vox Amoris" among all the love-poems of the world. Does the dear old purblind *Athenæum* know anything about this real poet, who has perhaps not been "discovered" by Mr. Grant Allen or Andrew Lang? Cheer up, old *Athenæum*, put on thy spectacles, and look about for the author of these "Litanies," lest the outer world should say thou art napping! People are reading "A Lover's Litanies"—those people who do not know anything about William Watson.

Robert Louis Stevenson started as a "poet," I believe. Now he has become the "Thucydides of literature"—*vide Pall Mall Gazette*. Such nice, pretty classical names the *Pall Mall* discovers for its particular darlings. Has the *Pall Mall* read Thucydides? I rather doubt it. I have, and find no resemblance to Mr. Stevenson. And, truth to tell, I preferred Mr. Stevenson's past poetry to his present prose. Yet why should I murmur, remembering the sweet, sound slumber into which I fell over "The Wrecker"—that trying mixture of Marryat and Clark Russell. I think it is a capital story for schoolboys though, and that is why the *Pall Mall* admires it. I am not a schoolboy; the *Pall Mall* is; a dear, bright, gamesome, peg-top-and-marble creature, who thinks the greatest joke in life is to break a neighbour's window or ring a neighbour's bell, and then run away laughing. Its animal spirits are too delightfully boisterous for it to appreciate any sort of deep sentiment; a story of strong human passions, or a romance in which love has the most prevailing share, would not appeal to its unlessoned fancy. And, very naturally, it appreciates Stevenson, because he gives it no hard, uncomfortable life-problems to think about.

Another "poet" who calls himself so is Hall Caine. He says the "Scapegoat" is not so much a novel as a drama, and not so much a drama as a "poem." Very good indeed! Excellent fooling, upon my life. Hall Caine can be very funny if he likes, though you wouldn't think it to look at him. When he called his story of the "Bondman" a "New Saga," it was only his fun. His wit is quite irrepressible. Among other humorous things, he has had his portrait taken in a loose shirt and knickers, seated facing the bust of Shakespeare, like a day-labourer fronting the Sphinx. It is altogether refreshing to find a Lilliputian literary ephemera so entirely delighted with himself as Hall Caine. He is much more convinced of the intrinsic value of his own genius than Oscar Wilde, with less reason than Oscar for his conviction. Oscar is a really clever man; Hall Caine tries to be clever and does not succeed. Oscar is a born wit, moreover, and though he does crib a few *bon-mots* from Molière and a few paradoxes from Rochefoucauld, what does it matter for the English who do not understand French, and have to get "books of the words" in order to "follow" Sarah Bernhardt. Besides, Hall Caine borrows from the French also; the plot of his "Scapegoat" is taken from the French, so one of my critical friends assures me, and critics are always right. Francis Adams (also a "poet") "went" for Hall Caine not long ago in the *Fortnightly*—a regular good knock-down thrust it was, too. But Adams's prowess is of no avail in these things. The more you abuse a fellow, the more his books sell. The best way to utterly damn an author is to say that his novels are "nicely written," "prettily told," "harmless fiction," or "innocuous literature." If these phrases do not finish him off, nothing will. An original, powerful, passionate writer is always "slated," and always "sells." Witness the career of one Emile Zola. With all his faults, the man is a great poet; realism and romance unite in strange colours on his literary palette, and with his forceful brush he paints life in all its varied aspects fearlessly and without any regard for outside opinions. His one blemish is the blemish of the whole French nation—moral Nastiness. But if we talk of "poets" who, though making their bread-and-butter out of the writing of prose, still insist on belonging to the gods of Parnassus, none of the stringers of rhyme and jinglers of ballads, and weavers of "sagas" and the like, that afflict this enlightened and imaginative nation, could write such a true poem from end to end as "Le Rêve." Such consummate art, such unravelling of exquisite romance out of commonplace material, is not to be discovered in the English literary brain. The English literary brain is dull, lumpish, and heavy—the English literary worker is dominated by one idea, and that is, how much hard cash shall he get for his work? And thus it is that poets, real poets, are rarer than swallows in snow; so that is why I am slightly exercised in my mind respecting the Petrarch sort of minstrel I spoke of a while ago. He is unquestionably a poet, and seems to get on without any "booming." This strikes me as very odd. However, most of the "best" men go unboomed. No occasion to puff a good article. As for the pretended poets, countless as the sands of the sea, there is a great consolation in the reflection that in a few more years they will all be as though they never had been. Good old Posterity will know nothing about them, and herein Posterity is to be heartily congratulated. Poetical gnats must live like other gnats, I suppose— they are rather troublesome, and make a buzzing noise in one's ears, but as their whole existence lasts no more than a day, we must have patience till the sun sets.

XVI

To a Mighty Genius

"O Rudyard Kipling! Phœbus! What a name,
To fill the speaking trump of future Fame!"

This, with apologies to the shade of the "loose ungrammatical" Byron, as the perfectly grammatical Gosse calls him. Dear Gosse! He has cause to be somewhat irritated with his own career as a poet, for he has not yet "set the Thames on fire," as he expected to do with the torch of his inspiration. Hence he was compelled to vent his pent-up spleen somehow, and what better dead giant to fall upon and beat with pigmy blows of pigmy personal vexation than Byron, whose Apollo-like renown (with scarce an effort on his own part) sent thunders through Europe. Oh, grammatical Gosse!—but never mind him just now; I must concentrate my soul on Kip; on Rudyard; on the glory of this literary age. Let me look at you, you blessed baby! treasure of its own Grandmother Journalism's heart! There you are, crowing and chuckling, small but "virile," every inch of you, though you are not overstocked with hair on the top of that high head of yours, and it is hard to begin life by viewing it through spectacles. But *as* you are, there you are! and my pulses leap at the sight of you. Fielding, Sterne, Thackeray, Dickens, all these parted spirits have, as it were, distilled themselves into a fiery fluid wherewith to animate your miniature form; was ever such a thrilling wonder? Hear we good Uncle *Blackwood*, the while he dances you upon his gouty knee:—"If her Majesty's Ministers will be guided by us (which perhaps is not extremely probable; yet we confess we should like the command of a Minister's ear for several shrewd suggestions) they will bestow a Star of India without more ado upon this young man of genius who has shown us all what the Indian Empire means."

No doubt, good 'nuncle! no doubt the Ministry will listen to thy "shrewd suggestions" what time the moon is made of ripe green cheese. Go on, old man, go on, in thy cracked and aged pipe, growing wheezy with emotion. "The battle in the 'Main Guard' is like Homer or Sir Walter. . . If her Majesty herself, who knows so much, desires a fuller knowledge of her Indian Empire, we desire respectfully to recommend to the Secretary for India that he should place no sheaves of despatches in the royal hands, but Mr. Rudyard Kipling's books. . . What Mr. Rudyard Kipling has done is an imperial work, and worthy of an imperial reward!"

Bravo, worthy 'nuncle! Homer begged his bread, but the pen-and-ink sketcher of "Mrs. Hauksbee" shall have rewards imperial! To it again, garrulous 'nuncle—to it and cease not! "Here, by the dignified hand of Maga the ever young, we bid the young genius All hail! and more power to his elbow, to relapse into vernacular speech, which is always more convincing than the high-flown." Should it not have been written "to relapse into bathos," good 'nuncle? And beware of declaring thyself to be "ever young," for nothing lives that shall not grow old, and the younger generation already profanely dub thee "antiquated." Wipe thine eyes, Uncle *Blackwood*, polish thy spectacles, and set down our precious baby for an instant the while his other nurses, godfathers and godmothers, look at him, and speculate upon his probable growth.

Let us listen to the hysterical *D. T.* the while it raveth in strophes of gin-and-water:—"Mr. Rudyard Kipling is, and seems likely to remain, a literary enigma. Who can deny his strength, his virility, his dramatic sense, his imaginative wealth, his masterful genius? He is like a young and sportive Titan, piling Pelion on Ossa in his reckless ambition to scale Olympus; he is always renewing his strength like an eagle, and rejoicing like a giant to run his course. Nothing comes amiss to him; he will produce out of his boundless stores things new and old—tragedies, comedies, farces, epics, ballads, or lyrical odes. His earliest Anglo-Indian stories revealed a new world to the astonished West; his "Soldiers Three" have attained almost the reputation of the "Three Musketeers"; his Learoyd, his Ortheris, his Mulvaney, his Mrs. Hauksbee, his Torpenhow are household words; while his barrack-room ditties, and his ballads of East and West have not only startled by their daring frankness, but conquered all criticism by their picturesqueness and truth."

All this, an' so please you, on two or three volumes of small magazine stories and rhymed doggerel! That "Soldiers Three" should have attained the reputation of the "Three Musketeers" is of course only the delirious frenzy of the *D. T.* asserting itself in gasping shrieks of illiterate mindlessness—Europe knows better than to place the intellect of a smart newspaper man like Kipling on the same level with that of Dumas. Kipling is the Jumbo of the *D. T.* for the present, and journalists would not be what they are if they could not get up a "boom" somehow. Now hark we to the fond maudlin murmur of an evening journal!

"Where did Kipling get his ideas about Art from?" This is indeed a pathetic question. It crops up in a paragraph-ecstasy over "The Light that Failed." It is as if one should ask, "Where did Shakespeare get his knowledge of the human soul from?" Where, oh where? We cannot, we will not believe he has any imagination, this dear Kipling of ours, because imagination is a thing we abhor. The triumphal and eternal books of the world have all been purely imaginative, but this does not matter to us. We, in this modern day, refuse to accept the idea that anybody can describe a thing they have not seen and felt and turned over and over under a microscope; we are so exact. And oh, where then did Shakespeare (to revert to him again, because his is the only name we can conscientiously compare with Kipling), where did Shakespeare find Ariel and Caliban, and Puck and Titania, and Julius Cæsar, and Antony and Cleopatra? He could not have seen these people? No. Then, alas! he had that fatal gift, that monstrous blemish of the brain which spoils true genius, Imagination—the grossest form of cerebral disease. In this he was inferior to our Rudyard, our hop-skip-and-a-jump Rudyard, who is actually going bald in his youth from the strain of his minute observation of life, and the profundity of his meditations thereon. Our "delectable one!" Our precious Kip! Who would not join in the chorus of the paragraph-men when they propound the fond, almost maternally-admiring query, "Where did he get his ideas about Art from?" And then, when we find out that he has "artistic" relations; that his papa is, or has been, painting a ceiling or a wall in Windsor Castle, we naturally feel almost beside ourselves with delight, because we find our baby's ideas are the result of heritage, and have nothing to do with that curse of literature, Imagination. As for me, I weep whenever I turn the sacred leaves of "Plain Tales from the Hills," because I know I have in its pages all that ever was or will be excellent in the way of fiction. There is nothing more to be said—nothing more to come after. It is a sad thought that fiction should have culminated here—it is always sad to think that anything should have an end—but when the end is so glorious, who shall complain? And so I have sold my set of Waverley novels (the real Abbotsford edition); I have put my Shakespeare on an almost unreachable top shelf (I only keep him for reference); I have sent my Dickens volumes to a hospital, and my Thackeray to a "home for incurables." I shall not want these things any more. The only natural reflex of life as it is lived nowadays is to be found in the works of Rudyard; on Rudyard I mentally feed and thrive. To Kip I cling as the drowning sailor to a rope; all difficulties and perplexities in Art, Literature, Science, Politics, Manners and Morals vanish at the touch of his mighty pen—he is the one, the only Kip;—the crowning splendour of our time. Why should we make any parliamentary pother over the preservation of old buildings at Stratford-on-Avon? What do we want with Stratford-on-Avon? since our Kip was born in India, or we believe he was. Now, India is something like a place for a Genius to be born in—big, vast, legendary, historical—and yet the American Interviewer, conscious of Kipling's might, thinks it possible he may have already exhausted its capabilities for literary treatment; swallowed it off at one gulp as it were, like the precious pearl Hafiz consumed in his cup of wine.

"Do you consider Mr. Kipling has exhausted India?" anxiously inquired the American Interviewer of Rider Haggard, when the weary author of "She" landed in New York.

"India is a big place," was the simple answer, given with a patient gentleness for which Haggard deserves great credit, seeing how he has lately been despitefully used and persecuted by the very reviewers who once flattered him.

Yes, India *is* a big place; not too big for our Kip though. He requires to take life in Gargantuan gulps in order to support the giant forces of his mind. But Stratford-on-Avon! A mere English country town— hardly more than a village—what do we care about it now? Shakespeare, after all, was perhaps only Bacon—but Kip is Kip—there's no doubt about him—he is his own noble *bonâ-fide* self, whose bootlaces we are not worthy to untie. There is "stern strength," there is "virility," there is a "strong strain of humour," there is "masculine vigour" in everything he writes. Mark the following passage from "Watches of the Night":—

"Platte, the subaltern, being poor, had a Waterbury watch and a plain leather guard.

"The Colonel had a Waterbury watch also, and for guard the lip-strap of a curb chain."

Now, note that carefully—"*The lip-strap of a curb chain.*"

What a luscious flowing sound there is in those few exquisitely chosen words! "*The lip-strap of a curb chain!*" It is positively fascinating. One could dream of it all day and all night too, for that matter, like Mark Twain's famous refrain of "Punch in the presence of the passenjare." But going on from this delicious line, which is almost poetry, one finds instant practical information.

"Lip-straps make the best watch-guards. They are strong and short. Between a lip-strap and an ordinary leather guard there is no great difference; between one Waterbury watch and another, none at all."

Now, there we have the "strain of humour." No difference between one Waterbury watch and another, "none at all." Ha, ha, ha! No difference between one—ha, ha, ha!—Waterbury, ha, ha!—watch—ha, ha, ha!—and another—ha, ha, ha!—none at all. Ha, ha! That "none at all" is so exquisitely facetious! It comes in so well! Was ever such a delightful little bit of sly, dry, brilliant, sparkling Wit, with a big W, as this peculiar manner of our Kip! Turning over the leaves of this glorious, this immortal "Plain Tales," you cannot help coming upon humour, spontaneous, rollicking humour everywhere. It bristles out of each particular page "like quills upon the fretful porcupine." Take this, for example—

"One of the Three men had a cut on his nose, caused by the kick of a gun. *Twelve-bores kick rather curiously.*"

So they do. The remarkable part of this is that twelve-bores *do* kick—it is a positive fact—a fact that every one has been dying to have made public, and "rather curiously" is the exact expression that suits their mode of behaviour. So true, so quaint is Kip. And here is another charming bit of expression—a descriptive picture, finely painted. It is from "The Arrest of Lieutenant Golightly."

"His boots and breeches were plastered with mud and beer stains. He wore a muddy-white, dunghill sort of thing on his head, and it hung down in slips on his shoulders, which were a good deal scratched. He was half in and half out of a shirt, as nearly in two pieces as it could be, and he was begging the guard to look at the name on the tail of it."

Now this requires thinking over, because it is so subtle. The "muddy-white, dunghill sort of thing" is really a new expression—quite new—and beautiful. It suggests so much! But you must come to the humour—you must remember there was a shirt mentioned, and that the hero was "begging the guard to look at the name on the tail of it." I went off into positive convulsions of mirth when I first read that passage. Falstaff's coarse witticisms seemed unbearable after it. "To look at the name on the tail of it!" It is simply inimitable. There is a jovial sound in the very swing of the sentence. And Private Mulvaney! What a creation! Just listen to him—

"I'm a born scutt av the barrick-room! The Army's mate and dhrink to me, bekase I'm wan av the few that can't quit ut. I've put in sivinteen years an' the pipeclay's in the marrow av me. Av I wud have kept out av wan big dhrink a month, I wud have been a Hon'ry Lift'nint by this time—a nuisince to my betthers, a laughin' stock to my equils an' a curse to meself. Bein 'fwhat I am, I'm Privit Mulvaney wid no good-conduc' pay an' a devourin' thirst. Always barrin' me little frind Bob Bahadur, I know as much about the Army as most men."

No wonder, after this, that the ever-watchful purveyors of "Literary Gossip" rouse themselves up from lachrymose tenderness to positive passion *in re* this marvellous Rudyard, and speak of him as "the stronger Dickens going forth conquering and to conquer."

The phrase, "the stronger Dickens," is coming it very strong indeed, but—it's only the paragraph-men. These chroniclers of the time have pathetically informed us how on one occasion Kip ran away from the "clamour" (of the paragraph-men) to India to fetch his papa, and how his papa came back with him, to look after him, I suppose, and protect him from all the naughty, vicious people who wanted to blow his skin out into the size of a bull when Nature meant him to keep to the strict proportions of the other figure in the fable. Good Rudyard! Already the bloom is off the rye, just slightly, for if we are to believe the *Athenæum*, an Eden Phillpotts is "the new Kipling." "O Eden Phillpotts! Phoebus! What a name! To fill the speaking-trump of future Fame!" The "loose ungrammatical" Byron's lines fit Phillpotts as excellent well as Kipling. Phillpotts is really a fine name in every way—splendidly hideous, and available for all sorts of Savile Club and *Saturday Review* witticisms, such as—

> *"Phill the Pott and fill the can*
> *Eden is our Coming Man!"*

Or this, sung slowly with religious nasal intonation to the well-known hymeneal melody—

> *"The voice that breathed o'er* Eden,
> *From* Athenæum *bowers,*
> *Said 'Phillpotts' stories must be praised,*
> *He is a friend of ours!'"*

Think of it, Rudyard! think of it! Art ready to cope with Phil? Wilt meet Potts on his own ground? Deem not thyself Eden's superior, for he "understands," according to the *Athenæum*, "proportion, contrast, balance, and the value of unhalting movement," things that inferior persons like Scott, Thackeray, Balzac, and others had to study all their lives long. Moreover, another journal dictatorially announces that "novel-readers must prepare to welcome" Phillpotts. Mark that "must"! That "must" would fain seize the Ass-public by the throat, and make it eat Phillpotts like a turnip. But the Ass is a fastidious ass sometimes— it likes to nose its food before devouring; it will nose Phillpotts at its pleasure. Meantime, it is nosing thee, friend Kipling, dubiously and with a faint touch of derision. Ridicule kills; beware of it, my boy. And to avoid ridicule and secure dignity, hist!—a side-whisper, meant kindly—*Put down your Boom business!* Stamp it out. Hush it up. If you don't take my advice you'll regret it. The thing has been over-done. You have had more friends than are good for you; a few stanch foes would have brought you much more benefit in the long run. When your ill-advised flatterers quote your jingly "Barrack-Room Ballads" as though they were things immortal—when good Frank Harris, of *Fortnightly* prowess, imposes a growling recital of scraps of your doggerel, "Fuzzy-wuz," on patiently-bored people sitting at a social meal, with the air of one considering it a finer production than "The Isles of Greece," or Shelley's "Cloud"—we say with Hamlet, "Somewhat too much of this." In the year of grace 1900 "Barrack-Boom Ballads" will have gone the way of all "occasional verse," and not a line will remain in the memory of the public. The English people know perfectly well what poetry is, and no critic will ever persuade them that you can write it. At the same time no one wishes to deny your surface cleverness or your literary ability. You are on the same rank with Bret Harte, Frank Harris, Frank Stockton, Anstey, and a host of others, and there is no objection taken to your standing along with these; but there is objection, honest objection, made to your being forced higher aloft than your compeers, by means of a ridiculously exaggerated, aggressively ubiquitous "boom." When Walter of the *Times* rushed frantically into a court of law about his copyright in a Kipling article (he having taken no such heed of any other author's article till then), the outside public laughed and shrugged their shoulders at the absurdity of the thing. From the fuss made, one would have imagined that God Himself read the *Times* every morning, and was particularly interested in Kipling. This sort of nonsense never lasts. The reaction infallibly sets in. Never was a name sent up sky-high like a rocket, but it did not fall plump down like a stick. And so, excellent Rudyard, beware! You are not "the greatest English author" by a long way. In weak moments I admit that the newspaper-gushers work me into a delirium-tremens of ecstasy about you, and, like my friend Frank Harris, my hand trembles and my voice takes on a rich growl as I quote "Fuzzy-wuz" and the "immortal" (alas!) "Tomlinson"— but in these fits I am not answerable for my words or actions. When I put away "Plain Tales" and "Life's Handicap," and forget all your press notices, I can think of you calmly and quite dispassionately, as one literary labourer among hundreds of others, who are all striving to put their little brick into the building of the Palace of Art, and I perceive that yours is a very small brick indeed! I fear it will scarcely be perceived in the wall twenty years hence. And my present opinion of you is—would you care to know it? Of course not, but you shall have it all the same. I consider you, then, to be a talented little fellow with a good deal of newspaper-reporter "smartness" about you, and an immense idea of your own cleverness, an idea fostered to a regrettable extent by the overplus of "beans" which gentle Edmund Yates, among others, is sorry to have given you. You have some literary skill, and you use a rough brevity of language which passes for originality in these days of decadence, but you are shallow, Rudyard; as shallow as the small mountain brook that makes a great noise in the rapidity of its descent, but can neither turn a mill-wheel or bear a boat on its surface. Your men characters are mostly coarse bears—unmannerly ruffians in their speech at least—your women are, on the average, either trifling or despicable. Though unlovable, they are, however, interesting for the moment, but only for the moment. Because a good many of us know fellows who are brave and "virile" and all the rest of it, and yet who are not obliged to use a slang word in every sentence; and we also know women who are not solely occupied with the subjugation of the "masculine persuasion"; and we prefer these decent folk as a rule. But, whatever your literary failings or attainments, and however you may display them *in futuro*, be wise in time and put down your "boom." No man can live up to a "boom"; it is not humanly possible. As for your "strong strain of humour," I am disposed to accept that as a fact. It *is* a strain—your humour. Your hydraulic pump is for ever going, and if the result is not always witty, it is flippant enough. And flippancy passes for wit nowadays. "Chaff" has replaced epigram, except when one finds a *bon mot* in an old forgotten

French play or novel, and passes it off in English as one's own "to set the table in a roar." As a matter of fact though, human life is tragic; and the comedy part of it is only invented hurriedly and inserted by the clowns of the piece.

And now Kip—though I perceive you are staring at me, wondering who the d———l I am—I will e'en leave you to your own devices, and, as the police say, "move on." Not even with the aid of your spectacles can you peer through the folds of my domino—not till I choose. I am not going about masked always—oh no! You shall see me face to face one day. And if, when these attractive features of mine are unveiled to your ken, you find yourself at all put out by the familiar manner of my speech to you, why, we will cross the Channel to some convenient scene of action, and you shall order (if you like) pistols for two and coffee for one. I am really one of the best of your friends, because I do not flatter you. The only place on which my observations may hurt you is a soft spot in every man's composition called Conceit. It is a spot that bruises easily and keeps sore for a long period. But the true artist requires to have this spot taken out of him if possible. It is as bad as a cancer, and needs instant cutting. Again I say, I do not flatter you. And if I had more time, I think I should possibly warn you against one of *your* "boomers," and *my* dear friends, Daddy *Lang*-legs. He has the caprices of a fine lady, has Daddy—you can never be sure when he is going to be pleased or displeased. He may discontinue a promising young "boom" quite suddenly, or on the other hand he may go on with it for an indefinite period. Of course he is an adorable creature, only it is not prudent to judge the position of all Literature by the phases of his humour.

And so, ta-ta Rudyard! See you again by and by! Don't inflate that little literary personality of yours too much, lest it should burst. Don't you believe you are a "stronger Dickens"; it won't do. It's bad for you. A little modesty will not hurt you; it is an old-fashioned manner, but is still considered good form. Read and compare the greater authors who never were "boomed"; who starved and died, some of them, to win greatness; they who are the positive "Immortals," and whom neither you nor any of us will ever distance; mistrust your own powers and "go slow." If there is anything very exceptional in you, time will prove it; if not, why, Time will sweep you away, my good fellow, as remorselessly as it has swept away many another pampered and petted "Press" baby out of the very shadow of remembrance. Don't swallow *all* the "beans" my boy! Leave a few. Better die of starvation than surfeit!

XVII

Concerning a Great Fraternity

Ha! I spy a Critic. Hail fellow, well met! Whether you have a strawberry mark on your left arm or not, you are my own, my long, my never-lost brother. I love you as the very apple of mine eye! And to speak truly, I love all critics, from the loftiest oracle to the lowest half-crown paragraphist; they are dear to me as the fibres of my heart, and I am never so happy as in their company. And why? Why, because I am a critic myself; one of the mystic band; and, moreover, one of the joyous throng wearing (for the present moment) the safety-badge marked "Anonymous"; one of the pleasant personal friend-detectives who watch the unsuspicious author playing his game of literary "baccarat," and, on the merest hint, decide that he is cheating. I shake the unsuspicious author's hand, I break his bread, I drink his wine, I smoke his best havanas; I tell him verbally that he is a first-rate fellow, almost a genius, in fact, and then?—well, then I sneak cautiously behind the sheltering sidewall of a leading journal with the rest of my jolly compeers, and at the first convenient opportunity I stab him in the back!—"dead for a ducat." And how we all laugh when he falls, his foolish face turned up in dumb appeal to the callous stars; he was a star-gazer from the first, we say, chucklingly—these ambitious dunderheads always are!

By Heaven! there is nothing in all the length and breadth of literature so thoroughly enjoyable as the life of a critic, if one were only better paid. One is member of a sort of "*Vehmgericht*," or secret inquisition, where great intellects are broken on the wheel, and small ones escape scot free, not being dangerous. The only unfortunate thing about it is that we are losing power a little. The public read too many books, and begin to know too much about us and our ways, which is very regrettable. We like to toss together our own style of literary forage and force it down the gaping throat of the public, because somehow we have always considered the public an Ass, whose best food was hay and thistles. But our Ass has lately turned restive and frequently refuses to accept our proferred nourishment. It snorts dubiously at our George Meredith Eccentricity, it kicks at the phonographic utterances of Browning, and it positively bolts at Ibsen. A disgusting Ass, this public! It actually devours volumes we have decided to ignore—it relishes poems which We pretend never to have heard of—it tosses its head at novels which We recommend, and hangs fondly over those We abuse; and it even goes and fawns at the feet of certain authors who show unrestrained passion and idealism in their writings, and whom, on account of that very passion and idealism, we have determined to send to Coventry. My heart sank to zero on a recent occasion when the editor of the *Academy* said to me, despondently, "The time is past, my friend, when criticism can either make or mar an author's reputation." Good God! I mentally exclaimed; then what am *I*—what are *we*—to do? What becomes of our occupation? If we may neither stuff nor flay authors, where is our fun? And how are we to get our bread-and-butter? The selling of three-volume novels alone will not keep us, though we always add a little to our incomes by that business.

This is how we generally manage. A Three-volumer comes in "for review," nicely bound, well got up; we look at the title-page, and if it is by some individual whom we know to be a power in one or other of the cliques, we pay strict attention to it, cover its faults, and quote platitudes as epigrams. But if it is by some one we personally dislike, or if it is by a woman, we never read it. We simply glance through it in search of a stray ungrammatical sentence, a misprint, or a hasty slip of the pen. (The misprints we invariably set down to the author, as though he had personally worked the printing-press and muddled the type out of sheer malice.) We obtain a vague idea of the story by this means, and if we find the ungrammatical sentence or the slip of the pen we are happy— we have quite enough to go upon. We tuck our Three-volumer under our arm and make straight for a secondhand book-store (where we are known), and there we sell it, after somewhat undignified bargaining, for three or five shillings, perhaps more, if its author has any reputation with the public. Then we go home and write half a column of "smart" abuse about it, or what is worse, luke-warm praise, for which we are paid from about five shillings to half a guinea, which, added to what we have wrested out of our secondhand bookseller, makes a respectable little sum, particularly when we get many Three-volumers, and effect many sales. (Poverty-stricken editors who write all their "reviews" themselves, or get their young sons and daughters at home to do it to save their pockets, and who sell for their own advantage all the "books received," naturally make quite a decent thing out of it.) And we can take our money always with the holy consciousness of having done more than our duty.

Yet, considering the earnestness with which we go to work, we are really very miserably rewarded. We do not make half such big incomes as the authors we judge and condemn. I say this advisedly, because, as a positive fact, the men and women writers whom we most hold up to opprobrium are the wretches who make the most money. The very devil is in it! The poets we go out of our way to praise, our Oxford and Cambridge pets and our heavy men, don't "sell"; not as they ought to (in our opinion), by any manner of means. And then they come to us—these children of the Muse—and complain bitterly that certain Press-ignored fellows, who never had a "boom" in their lives, *do* sell. And it is all the fault of the Ass-public, and we are supposed to be responsible for the humours of the Ass. It is too bad. We cannot help it if the Ass persists in remaining idiotically ignorant of the astounding wisdom contained behind the thick skull and solemn brow of a certain dear and choice morsel of mannerism we know, who dwelleth at Oxford, and who is called by some of his disciples "A Marvel." Aye, a marvel so marvellous that he hath grown weighty with the burden of his own wonder. And the phrase "I wonder!" is a frequent and favourite murmur of this impassive phenomenon; this "leader" of an excessively narrow literary "set"—this true "heavy father" of the little low comedy of Clique. For the rest, his voice is mild and dreamy, his eyes reserved and bilious, his step as of one in doubt, who deems the morning come when it is yet but night. Of a truth he is a good and simple goose, well stuffed with savoury learning; but whether the world will ever benefit by the dish is a matter which only the world itself can decide. Personally, I like the "Marvel"; I know him for a harmless soul, a gentlemanly dull *poseur*, whose posing vexes no one and amuses many. Only I have ceased to try and "write him up," because I have read his classic novel, and having accomplished that daring and difficult feat I consider I have done enough.

Among the minor entertaining experiences in the life of a critic are the appeals made to one's "quality of mercy" by the tender green goslings in authorship, who fondly imagine that by a coaxing word, or a flattery delicately turned, they can persuade Us to praise them. I saw a young woman striving to beguile my friend Lang in this way on one occasion, using sundry bewitchments of eye and gesture for the accomplishment of her fell purpose, and I caught a fragment of her soft yet desperate petition. "I am sure you will say a good word for my poems, Mr. Lang!" Her poems! ye gods and goddesses! A woman's poems, and—Andrew

Lang! Surely a Mephistophelian "ha, ha, ha!" rang out in the infernal regions of log-rolling at such a ridiculous combination, for when ever did the "Sign of the Ship" wave hopeful encouragement to a female rhymester? No, no; Lang, like myself, must know better than to give any foothold to the "vapid" feminine climber who wantonly attempts to scale Parnassus (a mountain exclusively set apart for the masculine gender), and threatens to overcome our "intensely moving, intensely virile stern strength;" *vide* publisher's advertisements of our ever-glorious Kipling.

Another curious feature of the critical disposition is our rooted dislike to be known as critics. In this we somewhat resemble those dear old robbers of legendary lore who went out pillaging and murdering merrily by night, and were the most perfect fine gentlemen in the daytime. Such altogether fascinating fellows they were! But we play our parts almost as cleverly, and I am sure with quite as much ease and charm. In polite society we claim to be "literary men"; the term is delightfully vague and may imply anything or everything. Some of us, however, say boldly out and out that we are not critics, but poets—*i.e.*, not judges, but criminals. We feel quite proud and glad when we have said this sort of thing. Take my amiable acquaintance, William Sharp, for instance. *He* says he is a poet, and he has a most refreshingly ingenuous and positive faith in his own statement. Few agree with him, but what does that matter, provided he is happy? Then there is Edmund Gosse; he also says he is a poet, and so he is, in a pretty daff-a-down-dilly, lady-like fashion. Only he sits as critic on other poets occasionally, and, strange to say, is never able to find anything in their productions quite equal to the sounds once evoked from "Lute and Viol." "Young" McCarthy, Justin Huntly (he is only called "young" lest he should be mistaken for "old"), he who uttereth oracles concerning plays and playwrights, he not only says he is a poet, but he once went so far as to call himself Hafiz—Hafiz in London. Yes; very much in London. Between the real Hafiz and the sham is a "great gulf fixed," and the ghost of the Persian singer is more valuable to literature than all the McCarthy substance. Now as to Edwin Arnold—Sir Edwin Arnold, C.S.I. (it never does to forget his C.S.I.), the admirer of those pretty ladies whose portraits appear on tea-trays—is he a poet?—is he a critic? Well, some of his own verses were described in the journal with which he is, or used to be, chiefly connected, *i.e.* the *Daily Telegraph*, as "the finest things that had appeared since the New Testament." Now, I consider this pretty strong, and I don't wish to comment upon it. If such an eulogy had been uttered by some other newspaper we should have said that the reviewer was some unduly excited personal friend who wanted to "use" Edwin afterwards for his own private purposes, but in the *Daily Telegraph*, C.S.I.'s own pulpit, it suggested—no matter what! Anyway, I am quite sure Edwin was not in Japan at the time.

I come now to another point in our careers as critics, and not such a very pleasant point either. We are the victims of toadyism. The little men of the Press, the dwarfs of journalism, toady us to the verge of distraction, as soon as we attain to Half-a-Guinea-a-Column power. Of course we are really somebodies then, and we have to pay the penalty of greatness. Still it is a bore. We are told all sorts of things that we know are not true, concerning our "fine literary abilities," our "keen discrimination," and our "quiet humour," but we are perfectly aware all the time that such "flattering unction" is merely the distilled essence of the most strongly concentrated humbug. No sane man, unless he has some private end in view which he hopes to gain by blandishment, would dream of giving us credit for "fine literary abilities," because if we had such abilities we should be doing something more paying than criticism. But our pigmy flatterers think we can swallow anything. Here is a small specimen of what I call Press-toadyism, which was bestowed on my dearest Andrew in *Galignani's Messenger* by somebody calling himself a *London Correspondent*. It purported to be a "review" of that amazingly dreary production, "The World's Desire," which, whatever its faults, had at least the effect of showing the joint authors thereof exactly what position they occupied as compared to Homer. Otherwise they might possibly have made some mistake about precedence. And thus ran the glib remarks of the *London Correspondent*:—

"That some parts are well written (Mr. Lang's) and some badly written (Mr. Haggard's), and that fights are many and blood is plentiful, and that there are many bits of delightful verse (Mr. Lang's, of course), and a cackling old person (the invention of Mr. Haggard evidently);" but there! I need not go on. The inquisitive individual who yearns to read the whole so-called "critique" can refer back to *Galignani* of December 8, 1890. The gratuitous and unnecessary insolence to Mr. Haggard, and the equally unnecessary and gratuitous licking-of-the-boots of Mr. Lang must have been decidedly offensive to both authors. This *London Correspondent* may be a man, but he certainly is not a brother.

Apropos of the subject of Press-toadyism, *in re* my friend Andrew, I must not forget here to chronicle my boundless admiration for that elaborate and beautiful witticism once contained in the *Saturday Review*. Criticising Andrew's "Essays in Little," the *Saturday* said:— "The public may like Little, but they certainly prefer it Lang!" *O mirabile dictu!* Shade of Joe Miller, retire discomfited! Was ever heard the like? What are the quips and cranks of a Yorick compared to this? Poor and feeble are the epigrammatic sentences of Molière; miserable to the verge of bathos every "happy thought" beside this sparkling production of the *Saturday*; this scintillating firework of atticism, launched with so much delicacy! Let me wipe my fevered brow, moist with the dews of ecstasy; I had always hoped the *Saturday* might one day be witty, but I never thought to see the fond anticipation realised. "Moribund," quotha? Never was the Jumbo of Reviews so frisky or so full of life before! Glorious old *Saturday Slasher*! As our American cousins say, "*Lang* may you wave!" Whoever perpetrated that delicious conceit on Andrew—Andrew, the very Pythias of my Damon worship—let him look me up at the Savile Club, and if I am there when he chances to call, he shall have such wine and welcome as can only be offered by a Critic with cash to a Critic of humour!

XVIII

Eulogiseth Andrew

In speaking of Andrew I wish it to be very distinctly understood that there is only one Andrew; and he is "the" Andrew as pronouncedly and positively as "the" Mactavish or "the" Mackintosh. He is, to use the words of the old Scottish song, "Lang, Lang, Lang a'comin'," always "a'comin'" it in every English printed journal and newspaper under the sun. His finger is in every literary pie. His shrill piping utterance is even as the voice of Delphic oracles, pronouncing judgment on all men and all things. He is the Author's Own Patent Incubator. His artificial warmth hatches all sorts of small literary fledglings who might otherwise have perished in the shell; and out they come chirping, all fuss and feathers, with as much good stamina as though they had been nursed into being under the wings of that despised old hen, Art. Andrew is better than Art, because he is the imitation of Art, and he comes cheaper than the real article. The way in which the old hen hatches her chicks is slow and infinitely laborious; the Lang Patent Incubator does the work in half the time and ever so much less worry. If you can only manage to place a literary egg close enough to the Incubator for him to "take notice" as it were, why there you are; out comes a chuckling author immediately and begins to pick his food from the paragraph-men with quite an appetite. He is quite a curious and wonderful institution in literature, is my dear Andrew. The pensters have had all sorts of things "occur" to them in their profession, such as "booms," "blackmail," "puffs," "burkings," "cliques," "literary societies," and the like, but I believe it has been left to our time to produce a literary Incubator. Of course Art goes on hatching strange birds in her own tedious and trying way— birds that soar sky-high and refuse paragraph-crumbs—but then they are a special breed that would have died of suffocation in the Lang Incubator. And they are a troublesome sort of fowl at best; they will never fly where they are told, never sing when they are bidden, and are never to be found scratching up dust in the press-yard by any manner of means. Now the Incubator produces no wild brood of this kind. He hatches excellent tame chicks, who make the prettiest little clucking noise imaginable, and scratch among the press-dust with grateful and satisfied claws, the while they prune each other's feathers occasionally with the tenderest "Savile" solicitude. Even timid spinsters could take up such pretty poultry in their aprons without harm. There are no horrible, snapping, strong-winged eagles among them? Lord bless you, no! Andrew would never be bothered with an eagle. It might bite his nose off! Eagles—*i.e.*, geniuses—are detestable creatures; you never know where to have them. And the Incubator must know where to have his chicks, else how could he look after them? Besides, geniuses always cause disaster and confusion in the press-yard—they find fault with the food there, and object to roost on the critically appointed perches. Fortunately, however, they are rare; and when Art does let loose such big troublesome chickabiddies the world generally lets them forage for themselves. Andrew certainly never troubles his head about them—indeed, he does his best to forget the unpleasant fact that they are flying about and might at any moment pounce on his "yairdie" and make havoc of his own carefully-incubated little literary brood.

Needless to say I am devoted to Andrew. He has done me the greatest kindness in the world. He does not know how kind he has been; in fact, he has such an open, guileless disposition that I believe he is quite unconscious of the heavy debt of gratitude I owe him. I have often thought I would try to express my sentiments towards him in some way, but my emotions have choked me, and I have refrained. Besides, great souls do not require to be thanked, and Andrew has a great soul. A great soul and "brindled hair." These qualities make him what he is, worthy of the admiration of all true Scots and inferior men. And of the "inferior" I will stand second to none in Lang-worship. Have I not followed him at a respectful distance when he has started off to rummage old bookstalls in search of literary provender? And have I not always admired the "pawkie" manner in which he has fathomed the childlike ignorance of the British public? For are not the contents of the books he picks up secondhand, forgotten, or unknown by the British public? and is it not well and seemly that he, Andrew, should revive them once more as specimens of pure Lang wit and wisdom? Certainly. No one would do the Incubator the hideous injustice of imagining him to be capable of any new ideas. New ideas have from time immemorial been an affront and an offence to the reviewer, and Andrew is not only a reviewer himself but the friend of reviewers. New ideas are therefore very properly tabooed from his list. But for old ideas, carefully selected and re-worded, no one can beat Andrew. He is a wandering "complete edition" of ideas taken from "dead" as well as living authors. As for poetry, I don't suppose any one will dispute the right he has to the Laureateship. The stamp of immortality rests on "Ballads in Blue China"—that same immortality which attends Kipling's "Barrack-Room" marvels. These things will be read what time future generations ask vaguely, "Who was Tennyson?"

Yes, Andrew, it is even so. You are a great creature, and a useful creature too, because you can turn your hand to anything. You are not dominated by any cerebral monomania. You are a Press jack-of-all-trades, and, like G. A. S., could write as smartly about a pin as about a creed. It is very clever of you, and I appreciate your cleverness thoroughly. I have had the patience to listen to some lectures of yours, sitting at your feet as at the feet of another Gamaliel, drinking in the wisdom of the secondhand bookstalls without a murmur. Only the most intense admiration of your qualities could have made me do that. I have even managed to spell out some of your calligraphy, which resembles nothing so much as the casual pattern which might be made by a spider crawling on the paper after having previously fallen into the ink. That was a feat performed in your honour—a feat of which I am justly proud. Then again I shall always love you for your frankly-open detestation of literary females. Females who presume to take up our writing weapons—and use them almost as well as we do ourselves—these are our pet aversion. We hate scribblers in petticoats, don't we, good Andrew? Yea, verily! We loathe their verses, we abominate their novels; we would kick them if we dared. We do kick them, metaphorically, whenever we can, in whatever journals we command; but that is not half as much as we would like to do. Almost we envy Hodge who can (and does) give an interfering woman a good dig in the ribs with his heavy hob-nailed boot whenever she provokes him; and in the close competition for literary honours we would fain be Hodges too, every man-jack of us. It is an absurdity that should not be tolerated in any civilised nation, this admission of women into the literary profession. What has she done there? What will she ever do? Ask Walter of the *Times* (he is a great authority) what he thinks of women who write. He will tell you that they are merely the weak imitators of men, and that they are absolutely incapable of humour or epigram. And I am convinced he is right. Mrs. Browning, Charlotte Brontë, Georges Sand, George Eliot, and others whose names assume to be "celebrated," are really nobodies after all. Walter of the *Times* could himself beat them out of the field—

if he liked. But he is too mercifully disposed for this: he reserves his genius. Sparkling all over with witticism, he only permits occasional flashes of it to appear in the columns of his magnificent journal, lest the public should be too much dizzied and dazzled. No wonder the *Times* costs threepence; you could not expect to get even a glimpse of a man like Walter for less. We ought to be glad and grateful for his opinions at any price.

And these epithets "glad" and "grateful" occur to me as the only suitable terms to apply to you, most super-excellent Andrew; my good friend to whom I owe so much. I am glad and grateful to know that your "lang" personality is a familiar object at so many newspaper offices. I am delighted to feel that English literature would come to a dead halt without your pleasantly long finger to push it on. It rejoices my heart to realise what a power you are. I am lost in astonishment at the extraordinary collection of Lilliputian authors you have hatched by your incubating process. They are the prettiest little brood imaginable, and what is so charming about them is that they are all so tame and well-behaved that they will never fly. This is such a comfort. Just a little scurrying and flopping through the press-yard is all they are capable of, and quite enough too. Comfortable hencoop sanity in literature is the thing; we don't want any of Professor Lombroso's maniacs in the way of geniuses about. They are dangerous. They do strange things and break out in strange places, and often succeed in stopping all the world on its way to look at them. Nothing would alarm you so much, I assure you, my dear Andrew, as the involuntary hatching of a genius. In fact, I believe it would be all over with you. You could not survive.

But, thanks to a merciful Providence, you run no risk of this. The old hen Art is a savage bird and lays her eggs among wild thorns and bracken out in the open, where no man can find them to bring to you for the artificial bursting heat of a "boom." You only get the dwarf product of the domestic poultry of the press-yard. And these are easily incubated by your patent process—in fact, they almost hatch themselves, they are in such a hurry to chirp forth their claims to literary distinction. But being fragile of constitution they need constantly looking after, which I should imagine must be rather a bore. Relays of paragraph-men have to come and throw corn and savouries all the while lest your little chicks should die of inanition, they having no stamina in themselves. Some will die, some are dying, some are dead; yet weep not, gentle Incubator, for their fate. It better suits thy purpose that such should perish, so long as thou dost remain to hatch fresh fowl upon demand. The press-yard relies upon thee for its stock of guaranteed male birds— its gifted "virile" roosters, whose "cocksure" literary crowings may wake old Granny Journalism at stated hours from too-prolonged and loudly-snoring slumbers; but produce no hens, Andrew, for if thou dost, thou art a mistaken patent and workest by a wrong process! Continue in the path of wisdom, therefore, and faithfully incubate only masculine fledglings for the literary coops. More we do not expect of thee, save that thou continue to be the king of compilers and the enemy of blue stockings. For myself, personally speaking, admiring thee as I am fain to do, I naturally implore thee to go on in all the magazines and journals telling me the things I knew before—the old stories I read when I was a thoughtless child, the scraps of information familiar to me as copybook maxims, the ancient jokes at which my elders laughed, the snatches of French romance and fable I picked up casually at school. For being always a book-lover it is but natural I should have learned the things wherewith thou instructest the ignorant world; but thou shalt tell me of them again and yet again, good Andrew, and yet I will not murmur nor ask of thee one thought original. Aware of all thou canst say, I still entreat thee, say it! Say it (to quote the jovial old *Saturday* once more) in "little," that I may have it "lang."

And now, ever famous and beloved Andrew, I must for the moment take my leave of thee. The glory of thy reputation is as a band of light around the foggy isles of Britain, and that benighted Europe knows thee not at all is but a trifle to us, though a loss to Europe. When Hall Caine recently found out that he was not celebrated in Germany he wondered thereat and said the Germans had no taste for English literature. No—not though they are the finest Shakesperian scholars in the world and the most ardent lovers of Byron's poesy. "Benighted Fatherland!" inwardly moaned the writer of "Sagas"—"Benighted country that knoweth not my works! Benighted people that have never heard—ye gods, imagine it!—have never heard the name of Kipling!" Oh, dull, beer-drinking, Wagner-ridden disciples of Goethe, Schiller, and Heine! To be ignorant of Kipling! To be only capable of a bovine questioning stare at Caine! To be impervious to the electric name of Lang! To know nothing about the new "Thucydides," R. L. Stevenson! Heaven forgive them, for I cannot. I abjure the Rhineland till it has been to school with Lang's text-books under its arm. Drop Heine, ye besotted slaves of "lager-bier," and read Kipling. *Try* to read him, anyway. If you can't, my friend Andrew will show you how. Andrew will show you anything that can be shown in English journals and newspapers. But beyond these he cannot go. You must not expect him to expand farther. His incubating work belongs solely to the English Press Poultry-yard—his name, his power, his influence avail, alas! as Nothing, out in the wide, wide world!

XIX

Byron Loquitur

If I did not believe, or pretend to believe, in Spiritualism, Theosophism, Buddhism, or some other fashionable "ism" which is totally opposed to Christianity, I should not be "in the swim" of things. And of course I would rather perish than not be in the swim of things. I cannot, if I wish to "go" with my time, admit to any belief in God; like Zola's Jean Bearnat, I say, "Rien, rien, rien! Quand on souffle sur le soleil ça sera fini," or, with the reckless Corelli, I propound to myself the startling question, "Suppose God were dead? We see that the works of men live ages after their death—why not the works of God?" The exclamation of "Rien, rien!" is *la mode*, and those who are loudest in its utterance generally take to a belief in bogies—Blavatsky bogies, Annie Besant bogies, Sinnett bogies, Florence Marryat bogies, many of which disembodied spirits, by the by, talk bad grammar and lose control over their H's. My jovial acquaintance, Captain Andrew Haggard (brother of Rider), and I, have rejoiced in the society of bogies very frequently. We have called "spirits from the vasty deep," and sometimes, if all the "influences" have been in working order, they have come. We know all about them. Haggard, perhaps, knows more than I do, for I believe he confesses to being enamoured of a rather pretty bogie—feminine, of course. She has no substance, so the little flirtation is quite harmless. I regret to say the "spirits" do not flirt with me. They don't seem to like me, especially since the Tomkins episode. The Tomkins episode occurred in this wise. At a certain *séance* in which I took a somewhat too obtrusive part a "bogie" appeared who announced himself as Tomkins. Some one asked for his baptismal name, and he said "George." A devil of mischief prompted me to hazard the remark that I once knew a John Tomkins, but he was dead.

"That's me!" said the bogie, hurriedly. "I'm John."

"How did you come to be George?" I demanded.

"My second name was George," replied the prompt bogie.

"That's odd!" I said. "I never knew it."

"You can't expect to know everything," remarked the bogie, sententiously.

"No, I can't," I agreed. "And, what is more, I never knew a Tomkins at all, John or George, living or dead! You are a fraud, my friend!"

Confusion ensued, and I was promptly expelled as an "unbeliever" who disturbed the "influences." And since that affair the "spirits" are shy of me.

Whether the memory of the Tompkins episode haunted me, or whether it was the effect of an excellent dinner enjoyed with "Labby" just previously, I do not know, but certain it is that on one never-to-be-forgotten evening I saw a ghost—a *bonâ-fide* ghost, who entered my sleeping apartment without permission, and addressed me without the assistance of a "medium." He was a ghost of average height and build, and I observed that he kept one foot very carefully concealed beneath his long, cloudy draperies, which were disposed about him in the fashion of the classic Greek. Upon his head, which was covered with clustering curls fit to adorn the brows of Apollo, he wore a wreath of laurels whose leaves were traced in light, and these cast a brilliant circle of supernatural radiance around him. In one hand he grasped a scroll, and as he turned his face upon me he beckoned with this scroll, slowly and majestically, after the style of Hamlet's father on the battlements of Elsinore. I trembled, but had no power to move. Again he beckoned, and his eyes flashed fire.

"My lord—!" I stammered, shrinking beneath his indignant gaze, and fervently hoping that I was not the object of his evident wrath.

"Lord me no lords!" said a deep voice that seemed to quiver with disdain. "Speak, puny mortal! Knowest thou me?"

Know him! I should think I did. There was no mistaking him. He was Byron all over—Byron, more thoroughly Byronic of aspect than any portrait has ever made him. Involuntarily I thought of the present Lord Wentworth and his occasionally flabby allusions to his "Grandfather," and smiled at the comparison between ancestor and descendant. My ghostly visitant had a sense of humour, and, reading my thoughts, smiled too.

"I see thou hast wit," he was good enough to observe in more pacific accents. "Hear me, therefore, and mark my every word! There are such follies in this age—such literary rascals, such damned rogues of rhymesters—oh, don't be startled! every one swears in Hades—that I have writ some lines and remodelled others, to suit the exigencies of the modern school of Shams. Never did Art stand at a premium in England, but God knows it should not fall to zero as it is rapidly doing. Listen! and move not while I speak; my lines shall burn themselves upon thy brain till thou inscribe and print them for the world to read; then, and then only, having done my bidding, shalt thou again be free!"

I bowed my head submissively and begged the noble Ghost to proceed, whereupon he unfolded his scroll, and read, with infinite gusto, the following:—

"ENGLISH SCRIBES AND SMALL REVIEWERS

"*Still must I hear? Shall* SWINBURNE *mouth and scream*
His wordy couplets in a drunken dream,
And I not sing, lest haply small reviews
Should dub me 'dead' and forthwith damn my muse?
No! My proud spirit shall not suffer wrong;
'Booms' are my theme—let satire be my song.

"*Through Nature's new-found gift, Magnetic skill,*
My soul obeys an influential Will,
And I from Hades rise to life again
To wield once more mine own especial pen,
Which none have rivalled in these sickly days
Of tawdry epics and translated plays,
When knavish cliques o'er honest Art prevail,
And weigh out judgment by the 'Savile' scale.
The petty vices of the time demand
Another scourging from my fearless hand;
Still are there flocks of geese for me to chase,
Still false pretenders to the 'poet's' place.
Who dare to pile detraction on my name,
Let such beware, for scribblers are my game!
Speed Pegasus! Ye modern pensters small,
WATTS, BRYDGES, MORRIS, ARNOLD, *have at you all!*
Remember well how once upon a time
I poured along the town a flood of rhyme
So strong and scathing that the little fry
Of rhymesters like yourselves were doomed to die!
Moved by that triumph past, I still pursue
The self-same road, despite the New Review
And Quarterly, *and other journals silly,*
That take dull articles by Mr. LILLY.

"Most men serve out their time to every trade
Save book-reviewers—these are ready-made.
Crib jokes from Yankee journals, got by rote,
With just enough of memory to misquote;
Ignore all beauty; find or forge a fault;
Revive old puns and call them 'attic salt';
Then to the 'Speaker' or to HENLEY go
(The 'pay' for book-reviews is always low);
Fear not to lie—'twill seem a ready hit;
Shrink not from blasphemy—'twill pass for wit;
Care not for feeling; launch a scurrilous jest,
And be a critic with the very best!

"Will any own such judgment? No, as soon
Trust wavering shadows 'neath th' inconstant moon,
Hope that a 'promised' critique will be done
By bland O'connor of the Sunday Sun,
Believe that Hodge's claims will ne'er increase,
Believe in GLADSTONE'S schemes for Ireland's peace,
Or any other thing that's false, before
You trust reviewers, who themselves are sore.
Never let thought or fancy be misled
By LANG'S cold heart or ALFRED AUSTIN'S head;
While such are censors, 'twould be sin to spare;
While such are critics, why should I forbear?
And yet so near these modern writers run
'Tis doubtful whom to seek and whom to shun,
Nor know we when to spare or where to strike,
The bards and critics are so much alike!

"To bygone times my lingering thoughts are cast;
Good taste and reason with those times are past!
Look round and turn each trifling printed page;
Survey the precious works that please the age;
This truth at least let satire's self allow,
No dearth of pens can be complained of now.
The loaded press beneath its labour groans,
And printers' devils shake their weary bones,
While ARNOLD'S epics cram the creaking shelves,

And KIPLING'S ballads shine in hot-pressed twelves
'New' schools of twaddle in their turn arise,
Where jingling rhymsters grapple for the prize,
And for a time these psuedo-bards prevail;
Each public 'library' assists their sale,
And, hurling lawful genius from its throne,
Takes up some puny idol of its own,
And judges Poesy as just a cross
'Twixt ASHBY STERRY, LANG, and EDMUND GOSSE.

"Behold! in various throngs the scribbling crew,
For notice eager, pass in long review;
Each spurs his jaded Pegasus apace:
Rhyme and romance maintain an equal race.
The Grand Old Paradox of Hawarden
Seizes in haste his too prolific pen,
And, heedless how the reading world is bored,
Thrusts to the front a MRS. HUMPHRY WARD,
With 'Robert Elsmere' frightened out of faith,
And 'David Grieve' a-prosing us to death;
Next trumpets CAINE'S 'integrity of aim,'
And gives to 'Mademoiselle Ixe' a name.
O Gladstone, Gladstone! 'Boom' it not so strong
Boomers may 'boom' too often and too long!
If thou wilt write on impulse, prithee spare!
More vapid authors were too much to bear;
But if, in spite of all thy friends can say,
Thou still wilt boomwards boom thy frantic way,
And in long articles to stupid papers
Thou still wilt cut thy literary capers,
Unhappy Art thy fresh intent may rue;
God save us, Gladstone, from thy next 'review'!

"Lo, the mild teacher of the Buddhist school,
The follower of the tamest blank-verse rule,
The simple ARNOLD, with his 'Asia's Light,'
Who wins attention by translation-right;
And both by precept and example shows
That prose is verse, and verse is merely prose,

Convinced himself, by demonstration plain,
There never will be such a book again,
And never such a 'marvellous proper' man
To charm the hearts of ladies in Japan!

"Who out at Putney on the common strays,
Unsocial in his converse and his ways?
'Tis SWINBURNE, the Catullus of his day,
As sweet but as immoral in his lay.
Grieved to condemn, the Muse must still be just,
Nor spare melodious advocates of lust.
Pure is the flame which o'er her altar burns;
From grosser incense with disgust she turns.
Mend, SWINBURNE, mend thy morals and thy taste;
Be warm, but pure; be amorous, but chaste;
Thy borrowed fancies to Villon restore,
And use old Scripture similes no more!

"Behold! ye cliques; one moment spare the text!
HALL CAINE'S last work, and worst—until his next!
Whether he drafts his 'sagas' into plays,
Or damns his brother authors with faint praise,
His elephantine style is still the same,
Forever turgid, and forever tame.
Boom for the 'Scapegoat'! it has been re-writ
To suit the measure of the critics' wit;
'Bondsman' and 'Deemster' tweak each other's toes,
And as a spurious 'genius' Caine doth pose,
Taking himself and all his books on trust,
And getting photographed with Shakespeare's bust!

"Another book of verses? Who again
Inflicts rhymed doggerel on the sons of men?
'Tis Orient KIPLING, the reviewers' boast,
The darling of the Anglo-Indian coast,
Who, on cheap praise and cheaper conquest bent,
Imports slang 'notions' from the soldier's tent,
And crams his lines with 'Tommy Atkins' here
And 'Tommy Atkins' diction everywhere—

'Barrack-Room Ballads!' come, who'll buy! who'll buy!
The precious bargain's low! 'i faith, not I!
For RUDYARD'S verse, despite his 'boom,' is flat,
Though critics bloat him with 'log-rollers' fat—
O RUDYARD KIPLING! Phoebus! What a name
To fill the speaking-trump of future fame!
O RUDYARD KIPLING, for a moment think
What 'chancey' profits spring from pen and ink!
Thy name already tires the public ear,
One shilling for thy 'Tales' seems monstrous dear;
For though they make a decent show of print
The book as book of worth has 'nothing in 't'.
O RUDYARD KIPLING! cease to scribble rhymes,
And stick to ARTHUR WALTER of the Times;
As 'Special Correspondent' or 'Our Own,'
But for God's sake leave Poesy alone;
Scratch not the surface of the mystic East
With flippant pen dipped in reporter's yeast,
For India's riddle is a riddle still
In spite of any 'Plain Tale from a Hill,'
The silent griefs of conquered tribes and nations
Are not explained in military flirtations,
Or 'ditties departmental,' trite of style,
(Any 'jongleur' could scrawl them by the mile;)
As 'Light that Failed,' thy race is nearly run,
Thy goose is cooked; thy stuffing's over-done!

"Lo, great 'Thucydides' of Samoa's isle
Relieves his inspiration and his bile,
And o'er the rolling ocean wide and deep
Sends the chef-d'œuvres that make his readers sleep.
The 'Wrecker' comes and ponderously heaves
O'er weary brains its soothing weight of leaves,
And those who never knew that joy before
Yield to the peaceful pleasure of the snore,
And drowse in chairs at clubs in open day,
Just as they drowsed o'er 'classic' 'Ballantrae.'
Hail to 'Thucydides'! and hail the pen
That writes him up above all other men;

　　　　　　　　　　MARIE CORELLI

For sleep's a blessing, and whate'er may hap
His works ensure a harmless, perfect nap.

"Lo, with what pomp the daily prints proclaim
The rival candidates for Attic fame;
In grim array though HAGGARD'S Zulus rise,
Yet 'Q' and dull GRANT ALLEN share the prize;
Then come the little train of 'Pseudonyms'—
A set of female faddists full of whims—
Who pour their vapid follies o'er the town,
Excusing Vice and sneering Virtue down;
Next see good BENTLEY'S list of writers small:
I wonder where the deuce he finds them all?
Some 'novel new' he issues every week,
A fiction of the kind that housemaids seek—
Mild tales of goose-love, which he thinks may please,
Sure only geese would purchase books like these!
Broughton's half-vulgar, half-lascivious stories,
And Mrs. Henry Wood's posthumous glories;
Here Madam TROLLOPE whirls her small 'Wild Wheel,'
There Mistress HENNIKER unwinds her reel,
And silly 'fictionists' of no repute
Spring up like weeds to wither at the root.
Excellent BENTLEY! stay thy lavish hand,
Continuous trash were more than we could stand;
Give us good authors who deserve their name,
And save thy once distinguished firm from shame;
Give prominence to Genius—publish less,
Or rivals new thy 'house' will dispossess,
In spite of folks who think the works of Shelley
Inferior to romances by CORELLI.

"GRANT ALLEN hath a 'heaven-sent' tale to tell,
But much he fears its utterance would not 'sell'
Wherefore, to be quite certain of his cash,
He writes (regardless of his 'inspiration') trash;
Practical ALLEN! Noble, manly heart!
Wise huckster of small nothings in the mart,—
To what a pitch of prudence dost thou reach

To feel the 'god,' yet give thy thoughts no speech,
All for the sake of vulgar pounds and pence!
God bless thee, ALLEN, for thy common sense!

"Health to 'lang' Andrew! Heaven preserve his life
To flourish on the sacred shores of Fife!
Prosper good Andrew! leanest of the train
Whom Scotland feeds upon her fiery grain;
Whatever blessings wait a 'brindled' Scot
In double portion swell thy glorious lot!
As long as Albion's silly sons submit
To Scottish censorship on English wit,
So long shall last thy unmolested rule,
And authors, under thee, shall go to school;
Behold the 'Savile' band shall aid thy plan
And own thee chieftain of the critic clan.
KIPLING shall 'butter' thee, and thou sometimes
Wilt praise in gratitude his doggerel rhymes,
And HAGGARD, too, thy eulogies shall seek,
And for his book another 'boom' bespeak;
And various magazines their aid will lend
To damn thy foe or deify thy friend.
Such wondrous honours deck thy proud career,
Rhymester and lecturer and pamphleteer,
Known be thy name, unbounded be thy sway,
And may all editors increase thy 'pay'—
Yet mark one caution ere thy next review
Falls heavy on a female who is 'blue.'
Grub-street doth whisper that a 'ladye faire'
Intends to snatch thee by the brindled hair
And stab thee through thy tough reviewer's skin
With nothing more important than a pin—
A case of 'table turned' and 'biter bit';
Heaven save thee, Andrew, from a woman's wit!

"What marvel now doth Afric's zone disclose?
A solemn book of rank blasphemous prose,
Writ by a MISTRESS SCHREINER, who elects
A Universal Nothing as her text;

Whereat the Athenæum, *doddering soul!*
Whimpers about the 'beauty of the whole,'
And shrieks, in columns of hysteric praise,
How such a work all nations should amaze:
'Nothing has ever been or e'er will be
Like Dreams'—produced by the blasphemous She;
So writes the Athenæum *to the few*
Who still pay threepence for a bad review,
And watch the hatching of the little plots
Conceived and carried out by Mr. Watts.
CHARLES DILKE! *Come forth from Mrs. Grundy's ban,*
And show thyself to be the 'leading' man,
With one strong effort snap thy social fetter
And get thy prosy journal managed better!

"Great Oscar! Glorious Oscar! Oscar Wilde!
Fat and smooth-faced as any sucking child!
Bland in self-worship, crowned with self-plucked bays,
Sole object of thine own unceasing praise,
None can in 'brag' thy spreading fame surpass,
And thou dost shine supreme in native brass.
Thou hast o'erwhelmed and conquered dead Molière
With all the mots *of* Lady Windermere;
Thou hast swept other novelists away
With the lascivious life of 'Dorian Gray.'
Thine enemies must fly before thy face,
Thou bulky glory of the Irish race!
Desert us not, O Wilde, desert us not,
Because the Censor's 'snub' 'Salome' got,
Still let thy presence cheer this foggy isle,
Still let us bask in thy 'æsthetic' smile,
Still let thy dwelling in our centre be;
England would lose all splendour, losing thee!
Spare us, great Oscar, from this dire mischance!
We'll perish ere we yield thee up to France!

"Wise HARDY! *Thou dost gauge the modern taste:*
Hence on man's Lust thy latest book is based—
A story of Seduction wins success,

Thus hast thou well deserved thy cash for 'Tess.'
Pure morals are old-fashioned—Virtue's name
Is a mere butt for 'chaff' or vulgar blame,
But novels that defy all codes and laws
Of honest cleanness, win the world's applause,
And so thy venture sails with favouring winds,
Blest with approval from all prurient minds.

"See where at HORSHAM, Shelley's muse is crown'd!
Two Parsons and a Justice on the ground!
What glorious homage doth 'Prometheus' win!—
Yet sure if ever parted ghosts can grin,
Wild laughter from the Styxian shores must wake
At such tame honours for the dead bard's sake;
An EDMUND GOSSE doth make the day's oration,
Oh, what a petty mouthpiece for a Nation!
And WILLIAM SHARP, face-buried in his beard,
Thinks his own works should be as much rever'd
As Shelley's, if the world were only wise
And viewed him with his own admiring eyes;
And LITTLE (Stanley) doth with GOSSE combine
To judge the perish'd Poet line by line,
Granting his 'lyrics' admirably done,
(Though they could match him easily, each one,)
But, on the whole, he filled his 'mission' well;
'Agreed!' says CHAIRMAN HURST, J.P., D.L.!

"O Shelley! my companion and my friend,
Brother in golden song, is this the end?
Is this the guerdon for thy glorious thought,
Thy dreams of human freedom, lightning-fraught?
No larger honours from the world's chief city,
Save this half-hearted, slow and dull 'Committee'?
Where Names appear upon the muster-roll
But only Names that lack all visible soul;
Conspicuous by his absence, TENNYSON,
The HORSHAM 'In Memoriam' doth shun;
Next, HENRY IRVING'S name doth much attract
(That 'glory' of the stage who cannot act)

But even he, the Mime, keeps clear away
From personal share in such a 'got-up' day,—
And not one 'notable' the eye perceives,
Save the Methusaleh of song, SIMS REEVES;
Alas, dear Shelley! Hast thou fallen so low?
And must thy Genius such dishonour know?
Is this the way thy Centenary's kept?
Better go unremembered and unwept
Than be thus 'celebrated' in a hurry,
And get 'recited' by an ALMA MURRAY!

"Now hold, my Muse, and strive no more to tell
The public what they all should know full well;
Zeal for true worth has bid me here engage
The host of idiots that infest the age
And spin their meagre prose and verse for hire,
Libelling genius if it dare aspire.
Let harmless BARRIE scrawl a Scottish tale
And English ears with 'dialect' assail,
Let WILLIAM ARCHER judge, and bearded SHARP
Condemn his betters, enviously carp
At living bards (if any), one and all,
Such is the way of versifiers small;
Let MORRIS whine and steal from Tennyson,
The poet King, whose race is nearly run,
Let ARNOLD drivel on, and SWINBURNE rave,
And godly PATMORE chant a stupid stave,
Let KIPLING, CAINE, and HARDY, and the rest,
And all the women-writers unrepressed,
Scrawl on till death release us from the strain,
Or Art assume her highest rights again;
Let HENLEY, to assert his tawdry muse,
Damn other bards by scurrilous reviews,
Feeding with rancour his congenial mind,
Himself the most cantankerous of his kind;
Let ANDREW LANG undaunted, take his stand
Beside his favourite bookstalls, secondhand;
Let 'Pseudonyms' appear in yellow pairs,
Let careful STANNARD sell her 'Winter' wares,

Let WATTS *'puff"* SWINBURNE, SWINBURNE bow to WATTS,
And Shakespeare be disproved by MRS. POTTS;
Let all the brawling folly of the time
Find vent in vapid prose and vulgar rhyme;
Let scribblers rush into the common mart
With all their mutilated blocks of art,
And take their share of this ephemeral day
With COLLINS and her 'Ta-ra-Boom-de-ay';
And what their end shall be, let others tell;
My time is up and I must say farewell,
Content at least that I have once agen
Poured scorn upon the puny writing men
That chaffer for the laurel wreath of fame,
And think their trash deserves a lasting name.
Immortal, I behold the passing show
Of little witlings ruling things below,
And smile to see, repeated o'er and o'er,
The literary tricks I lash'd before,
And lash again, with satisfaction deep;
And other 'rods in pickle' I shall keep
For those who on my memory slanders fling,
Envying the songs they have no power to sing!

"Gods of Olympus! Comrades of my thought,
Where is the fire that once Prometheus brought
To light the world? It warmed my ardent veins,
And still the nations echo forth my strains;
Greece still doth hold me as her minstrel dear
And decks with fragrant myrtle boughs my bier—
ENGLAND forgets—but England is no more
The England that our fathers loved of yore—
A huckster's stall—a swarming noisy den
Of bargaining, brutal, ignorant, moneyed men—
England, historic England! She is dead,
And o'er her dust the conquering traders tread,
Crowning with shameful glory on her grave,
Some greasy Jew or speculating knave;
While blundering GLADSTONE, double-tongued and sly,
Rules; the dread 'Struldbrug,' who will never die!

MARIE CORELLI

"Thus far I've held my undisturbed career
Prepared for rancour—spirits know not fear!
Catch me, a Ghost, who can! Who knows the way?
Cheer on the pack! The quarry stands at bay;
Unmoved by all the 'Savile' logs that roll—
I stand supreme, a deathless poet-soul—
Careless of LANG'S resentment, GOSSE'S spite,
SWINBURNE'S small envy, ARNOLD'S judgment trite,
HENLEY'S weak scratch, or Pall Mall *petty rage,*
Or the dull Saturday's *unlessoned page—*
Such 'men in buckram' shall have blows enough,
And feel they too are 'penetrable stuff,'
And by stern Compensation's law shall be
Racked on the judgment-wheel they meant for me!

"Adieu! Adieu! I see the spectral sail
That wafts me upwards, trembling in the gale,
And many a starry coast and glistening height
And fairy paradise will greet my sight,
And I shall stray through many a golden clime
Where angels wander, crowned with light sublime;
When I am gone away into that land
Publish at once this ghostly reprimand,
And tell the puling scribblers of the town
I yet can hunt 'boomed' reputations down!
Yet spurn the rod a critic bids me kiss,
Nor care if clubs or cliques applaud or hiss,
And though I vanish into finer air
The spirit of my Muse is everywhere;
Let all the 'boomed' and 'booming' dunces know
BYRON still lives—their dauntless, stubborn Foe!"

Enunciating the last two lines with tremendous emphasis, the noble Ghost folded up his scroll. I noticed that in the course of his reading he frequently repeated his former self, and borrowed largely from an already published world-famous Satire; and I ventured to say as much in a mild *sotto voce*.

"What does that matter?" he demanded angrily. "Do not the names of the New school of literary goslings fit into my lines as well as the Old?"

I made haste to admit that they did, with really startling accuracy of rhythm.

"Well, then, don't criticise," he continued; "any ass can do that! Write down what I have read and publish it—or—"

What fearful alternative he had in store for me I never knew, for just then he began to dissolve. Slowly, like a melting mist, he grew more and more transparent, till he completely disappeared into nothingness, though for some minutes I fancied I still saw the reflection of his glittering laurel wreath playing in a lambent circle on the floor. Awed and much troubled in mind, I went to bed and tried to forget my spectral visitor. In vain! I could not sleep. The lines recited by the disembodied Poet burned themselves into my memory as he had said they would, and I had to get up again and write them down. Then, and not till then, did I feel relieved; and though I thought I heard a muttered "Swear!" from some a "fellow in the cellarage," I knew I had done my duty too thoroughly to yield to coward fear. And I can only say that if any of the highly distinguished celebrities mentioned by the ghost in his wrathful outburst feel sore concerning his expressed opinion of them, they had better at once look up a good "medium," call forth the noble lord, and have it out with him themselves. I am not to blame. I cannot possibly hold myself responsible for "spiritual" manifestations. No one can. When "spooks" clutch your hand and make you write things, what are you to do? You must yield. It is no good fighting the air. Ask people who are qualified to know about "influences" and "astral bodies" and other uncanny bits of supernatural business, and they will tell you that when the spirits seize you you must resign yourself. Even so I have resigned myself. Only I do not consider I am answerable for a ghost's estimate of the various literary lustres of the age:—

> "Byron's opinions these, in every line;
> For God's sake, reader, take them not for mine!"

MARIE CORELLI

XX

Maketh Exit

The hour grows late, dear friends, and I am getting bored. So are you, no doubt. But though, as I said in the beginning, I take delight in boring you because I think the majority of you deserve it, I have an objection to boring myself. Besides, I notice that some of you have begun to hate me; I can see a few biliously-rolling eyes, angry frowns, and threatening hands directed towards my masked figure, as I leisurely begin to make my way out of your noisy, tumultuous, malodorous social throng. Spare yourselves, good people! Keep cool! I am going. I have had enough of you, just as you have had enough of me. I told you, when I first started these "remarks aside," that I did not wish to offend any of you; but it is quite probable that, considering the overweening opinion you have of your own virtues and excellencies, you are somewhat thin-skinned, and apt to take merely general observations as personal ones. Do not err in this respect, I beseech you! If any fool finds a fool's cap that fits him, I do not ask him to put it on. I assure you that for Persons I have neither liking nor disliking, and one of you is no more and no less than t'other. Loathe me an' you choose, I shall care little; love me, I shall care less. Both your loathing and your love are sentiments that can only be awakened by questions of self-interest; and you will gain nothing and lose nothing by me, as I am the very last person in the world to be "of use" to anybody. I do not intend to be of use. A useful person is one who is willing to lie down in the mud for others to walk dryshod over him, or who will amiably carry a great hulking sluggard across a difficulty pick-a-back. Now, I object to being "walked over," and if any one wanted to try "pick-a-back" with me, he would find himself flung in the nearest gutter. Wherefore, you observe, I am not "Christianly" disposed, and should not be an advantageous acquaintance. Though, if I were to tell you all the full extent of my income, I dare say you would offer me many delicate testimonies of affectionate esteem. Sweet women's eyes might smile upon me, and manly hands might grip mine in that warm grasp of true friendship which is the result of a fat balance at the banker's. But, all the same, these attentions would not affect me. I am not one to be relied upon for "dinner invitations" or "good introductions," and I never "lend out" my horses. I keep my opera-box to myself too, with an absolutely heartless disregard of other people's desires. I learned the gospel of "looking after Number One" when I was poor; rich folks taught it me. They never did anything for me or for anybody else without a leading personal motive, and I now follow their wise example. I live my life as I choose, thinking the thoughts that come naturally to me, my mind not being the humble reflex of any one morning or evening newspaper; so I am not surprised that some of you, whose opinions are the mere mirror of journalism, hang back and look askance at me, the while I pass by and take amused observation of your cautious attitudes through the eye-holes of my domino. Certes, by all the codes of social "sets" you ought to respect me. I am the member of a House, the adherent of a Party, and the promoter of a Cause, and your biggest men, both in politics and literature, know me well enough. I might even claim to have a "mission," if I were only properly "boomed"—that is, of course, if the Grand Old *Struldbrug*, as the irreverent ghost of Lord Byron calls him, Gladdy, were to rub his noddle against that of Knowles, and emit intellectual sparks about me in the *Nineteenth Century*. But I don't suppose I could ever live "up" to such a dazzling height of fame as this. It would be a wild jump to the topmost peak of Parnassus, such as few mortals would have strength to endure. So on the whole I think I am better and safer where I am, as an "unboomed" nobody. And where am I? Dear literary brothers and sisters, dear "society" friends, I am just now in your very midst; but I am retiring from among you because—well, because I do not feel at home in a human menagerie. The noise is as great, the ferocity is as general, the greed is as unsatisfied, and the odour is as bad as in any den of the lower animals. I want air and freedom. I would like to see a few real men and women just by way of a change—men who are manly, women who are womanly. Such ideal beings may be found in Mars perhaps. Some scientists assure us there are great discoveries pending there. Let us hope so. We really require a new planet, for we have almost exhausted this.

And now adieu! Who is this that clutches me and says, will I unmask? What, Labby? Now, Labby, you know very well I would do anything to please you; but on this occasion I must, for the first time in my life, refuse a request of yours. Presently, my dear fellow, presently! The domino I wear shall be flung off in your pleasant study in Old Palace Yard on the earliest possible occasion. Believe it! It would be worse than useless to try to hide myself from your eagle ken. The "lady with the lamp" on the cover of *Truth* shall flash her glittering searchlight into my eyes, and discover there a friendly smile enough. Meanwhile, permit me to pass. That's kind of you! A thousand thanks! And now, with a few steps more, I leave the crowd behind me, and, loitering on its outskirts, look back and pause. I note its wild confusion with a smile; I hear its frantic uproar with a sigh. And with the smile still on my lips, and the sigh still in my heart, I slowly glide away from the social and literary treadmill where the prisoners curse each other and groan—away and back to whence I came, out into the wide open spaces of unfettered thought, the "glorious liberty of the free." I wave my hand to you, dear friends and enemies, in valediction. I have often laughed at you, but upon my soul, when I come to think of the lives you lead, full of small effronteries and shams, I cannot choose but pity you all the same. I would not change my estate with yours for millions of money. Many of you have secured what in these trifling days is called fame; many others rejoice in what are pleasantly termed "world-wide" reputations; but I doubt if there is any one among you who is as thoroughly happy, as careless, as independent, and as indifferent to opinion, fate, and fortune, as the idle masquerader who has strolled casually through your midst, seeking no favours at your hands, and making no apologies for existence, and who now leaves you without regret, bidding you a civil "Farewell!"

Remaining in unabashed candour and good faith, one who is neither your friend nor enemy.

A Note About the Author

Marie Corelli (1855–1924), born Mary Mackay, was a British writer from London, England. Educated at a Parisian convent, she later worked as a pianist before embarking on a literary career. Her first novel, *A Romance of Two Worlds* was published in 1886 and surpassed all expectations. Corelli quickly became one of the most popular fiction writers of her time. Her books featured contrasting themes rooted in religion, science and the supernatural. Some of Corelli's other notable works include *Barabbas: A Dream of the World's Tragedy* (1893) and *The Sorrows of Satan* (1895).

A Note from the Publisher

Spanning many genres, from non-fiction essays to literature classics to children's books and lyric poetry, Mint Edition books showcase the master works of our time in a modern new package. The text is freshly typeset, is clean and easy to read, and features a new note about the author in each volume. Many books also include exclusive new introductory material. Every book boasts a striking new cover, which makes it as appropriate for collecting as it is for gift giving. Mint Edition books are only printed when a reader orders them, so natural resources are not wasted. We're proud that our books are never manufactured in excess and exist only in the exact quantity they need to be read and enjoyed.

bookfinity™

Discover more of your favorite classics with Bookfinity™.

- Track your reading with custom book lists.
- Get great book recommendations for your personalized Reader Type.
- Add reviews for your favorite books.
- AND MUCH MORE!

Visit **bookfinity.com** and take the fun Reader Type quiz to get started.

Enjoy our classic and modern companion pairings!